BRENDAN MCGINLEY & BRIAN CULLEN

MEN

NEW EDITION
250 MORE ESSENTIAL LISTS!

An Hachette UK Company
www.hachette.co.uk

New edition, first published in United States of America in 2013 by
Hamlyn, a division of Octopus Publishing Group Ltd
Endeavour House, 189 Shaftesbury Avenue
London WC2H 8JY UK
www.octopusbooksusa.com

The original *Top Ten for Men* was devised and created by Russell Ash

Design & layout copyright © Octopus Publishing Group Ltd 2013
Text copyright © Brendan McGinley & Brian Cullen 2013

Distributed in the US by Hachette Book Group USA
237 Park Avenue
New York NY 10017 USA

Distributed in Canada by Canadian Manda Group
165 Dufferin Street
Toronto, Ontario, Canada M6K 3H6

ISBN 978-0-60062-587-2
Printed and bound in China

10 9 8 7 6 5 4 3 2 1

CONTENTS

Introduction 12

Animals 14
Top 10 Most diverse nations, by monkey 14
Top 10 "Extinct" animals that were later rediscovered 15
Top 10 Deadliest man-eaters 16
Top 10 Tallest birds 17
Top 10 Largest cats 18
Top 10 Heaviest living reptiles 19
Top 10 Ghastly war animals 20
Top 10 Longest-living animals 22
Top 10 Fastest mammals 23
Top 10 Smartest animals 24
Top 10 Most venomous reptiles and amphibians 26
The 10 Cutest animals on the planet 27
Top 10 Longest dinosaurs 28
Top 10 Shortest non-avialan dinosaurs 29
Top 10 Hybrid animals 30
Top 10 Saber-toothed creatures 32

Sex 33
The 10 First Playboy Playmates of the year 33
The 10 Most recent Playboy Playmates of the year 34
Top 10 Highest-grossing NC-17 films 35
The 10 Most recent AVN female performers of the year 36
The 10 Most recent AVN male performers of the year 37
Top 10 Nations with the biggest population growth 38
The 10 Weirdest condom flavors 39
Top 10 Early adult video games 40–41
The 10 US states with highest HIV infection rate per capita 42
Top 10 Species with largest (erect) penis 43

TV & Film 44
Top 10 Longest-running TV shows 44
The 10 Longest-running first-run syndicated TV shows 45

Top 10 Films with the worst opening weekends 46
Top 10 Biggest film-opening weekends 47
Top 10 Highest-grossing movies that were never #1 48
Top 10 Highest domestic-grossing movies 49
The 10 Most useful Bruce Campbell one-liners 50
Top 10 Actors in highest-grossing movies 51
Top 10 Films with most Oscars 52
The 10 Lowest-rated "best motion picture" Oscar winners on metacritic 53
Top 10 Most profitable Pixar films 54
Top 10 Highest-grossing sports movies 55
Top 10 Highest-grossing superhero movies 56
Top 10 Highest-grossing movies released in 2012 57
The 10 Manliest Movies 58
Top 10 Longest films ever made 59
Top 10 Most expensive movies ever made 60
Top 10 Films of the 1980s 61

Internet 62

Top 10 Longest Wikipedia pages 62
Top 10 Most popular Twitter feeds 63
Top 10 Most popular science websites 64
The 10 Top humor websites 65
The 10 Top internet hoaxes 66
Top 10 Busiest websites in the USA 67
The 10 Lesser-known wikimedia projects 68
The 10 Greatest internet April Fool's pranks of 2012 69
Top 10 Most viewed Youtube videos of all time 70

Music 71

The 10 Top musicians with single stage names 71
Our 10 favorite bass solos of all time 72
Our 10 favorite guitar solos of all time 73
Our 10 favorite drum solos of all time 74
Top 10 Biggest-selling singles of all time 75
The 10 Top-selling albums of all time 76
Top 10 Most expensive guitars 77

Print 78
Top 10 Oldest written languages 78
Top 10 Bizarre book titles 79
The 10 Top pulp characters still in print 80
Top 10 Best-selling books of the 21st century 81
The 10 Most recent recipients of the Noble Prize for Literature 82
Top 10 Longest books ever written 83
The 10 Most recent Carnegie Medal winners 84
Top 10 Seldom-used English punctuation 85
Top 10 Fastest-growing magazine genres 86
The 10 Top comic creators who used pseudonyms 87

Visual Arts 88
Top 10 Most popular art exhibitions 2011 88
Top 10 Most expensive sculptures ever sold 89
Top 10 Most expensive photographs ever sold 90
Top 10 Most expensive paintings ever sold 91

Video Games & Applications 92
Top 10 Biggest video game conventions 92
Top 10 Best-selling video games of all time 93
Top 10 Highest-grossing arcade games 94
Top 10 Best-selling video game consoles of all time 95
Top 10 Best-selling video game franchises 96
Top 10 Most bizarre games merchandise created 97
Top 10 Best-selling handheld video game systems of all time 98
Top 10 Most popular free iphone apps ever 99
Top 10 Most popular paid-for iphone apps ever 100
Top 10 Most popular free ipad apps ever 101
Top 10 Most popular paid-for ipad apps ever 102
Top 10 Biggest MMORPGs 103

Automotive, Mechanical, & Travel 104
The 10 Top automakers worldwide 104
Top 10 Active longest US Route highways 105
Top 10 Highest-selling car models ever 106

The 10 Top iconic cars in movies and TV 107
Top 10 Earliest cars with three wheels 108
Top 10 Production car engines with the most cylinders 109
Top 10 Fastest active roller coasters 110
Top 10 Tallest active roller coasters 111
Top 10 Longest subway systems in the world 112
Top 10 First countries with railways 113
The 10 Top names for US military aircraft 114
Top 10 Busiest US airports 115
The 10 Worst peacetime marine disasters 116

Food 118
Top 10 Highest-grossing fast food chains in the USA 118
Top 10 US fast food chains with the most restaurants 119
Top 10 Best-selling US burger chains 120
The 10 Top beef-producing countries 121
Top 10 Animals most slaughtered for meat in the USA 122
Top 10 Fattest US states 123
Top 10 Skinniest US states 124
Top 10 Countries that eat the most fish 125
The 10 Top honey-producing countries 126
Top 10 Hottest chilis 127
The 10 US restaurants with 3 Michelin stars 128

Drink 129
Top 10 Beer-swillingest countries 129
Top 10 Biggest brewing companies by sales 130
The 10 Top craft beers 131
The 10 Most unusual ingredients found in specialty beers 132
Top 10 Beer with highest alcohol by volume 134
Top 10 Most bitter beers 135
Top 10 Most expensive beers 136
Top 10 Most expensive wines 138
Top 10 Most expensive bottles of tequila 139
Top 10 Most expensive scotches 140
Top 10 Most expensive vodkas 141

Top 10 Unfamiliar beer measurements 142
The 10 Oddest coffee flavors 144
Top 10 Most popular IPAs 145
Top 10 Largest green-coffee producers 146
Top 10 Best-selling soda brands 147
Top 10 Most expensive cigars in the world 148

Global 149
Top 10 Newest countries 149
The 10 Poorest nations by GDP (per capita) 150
Top 10 Most populated countries 151
Top 10 Smallest countries/sovereignties by population 152
Top 10 Countries spending the most on tourism 153
The 10 Biggest carbon dioxide polluters 154
Top 10 Longest-reigning monarchs 155
Top 10 Longest-reigning British monarchs 156
Top 10 Most widely spoken native languages 157
Top 10 Most popular tourist nations 158
Top 10 Countries that visit the USA most often 159
Top 10 Most powerful nuclear tests in the USA 160
The 10 Deadliest air disasters 161
The 10 Longest US war involvements 162

Federal 163
The 10 Tallest US presidents 163
The 10 Shortest US presidents 164
Top 10 Longest-serving US senators 165
Top 10 Longest-serving US representatives 166
The 10 Most recent Congressional Medal of Honor recipients 167
Top 10 Richest US states by household income 168
Top 10 Poorest US states by household income 169
Top 10 US states with the youngest population 170
Top 10 US states with the oldest population 171
Top 10 US states with most foreign-born residents 172
Top 10 US states with fewest foreign-born residents 173
Top 10 Least populous US states 174

Top 10 Most populous US states 175
Top 10 Biggest agricultural exporter US states 176

Municipal 177
Top 10 Oldest extant cities in the USA 177
Top 10 Most populous US cities 178
Top 10 Bizarre small-town slogans in the USA 179
Top 10 Quirky small town names in the USA 180

Money & Business 182
The 10 Most expensive private boats 182
Top 10 Largest lottery jackpots in the USA 183
The 10 Top oil-producing countries 184
The 10 Top oil-producing US states 185
The 10 Top silver-producing countries 186
Top 10 Most widely grown crops in the USA 187
Top 10 Countries that catch the most fish 188

The Natural World 189
Top 10 Newest periodic elements 189
Top 10 Most common metals in the human body 190
Top 10 Coldest days in US history 191
The 10 Hurricanes with strippers' names 192
Top 10 Wettest cities in the continental USA 193
The 10 Most expensive hurricanes in US history 194
The 10 Deadliest hurricanes in US history 195
The 10 Most recent retired hurricane names 196
Top 10 Closest stars 197
Top 10 Largest constellations 198
Top 10 Smallest stars in the known universe 199
Top 10 Largest stars in the known universe 200

Society & Humanity 201
Top 10 US states with highest birth rates 201
Top 10 US states with lowest birth rates 202
Top 10 Most popular baby names in the USA 203

Top 10 Largest US ancestries 204
Top 10 US religious beliefs 205
Top 10 Smallest multiple-church religions on record in the USA 206
Top 10 Leading causes of injury in the USA 207
The 10 Most annoying co-workers 208
The 10 Top cultural holidays celebrated in US 209
The 10 Self-made wealthiest women 210
Top 10 Verified oldest people 211
Top 10 Oldest people who lived in three centuries 212
Top 10 Countries with highest life expectancies 213
The 10 Countries with lowest life expectancies 214
Top 10 US states with highest male life expectancy 215
The 10 US states with lowest male life expectancy 216

Death & Disaster 217
Top 10 Extinction events 217
The 10 Top causes of death in the US 218
The 10 Leading causes of death worldwide 219
The 10 Deadliest US states for law officers 220
The 10 Deadliest US wars (by American fatalities) 221
The 10 Deadliest occupations in the USA 222
The 10 US states with highest mortality rates 223
The 10 US states with lowest mortality rates 224
The 10 Countries with most work fatalities 225
The 10 Deadliest coal mine disasters 226
The 10 Deadliest maritime disasters 227
The 10 Deadliest nuclear accidents 228
The 10 First space exploration casualties 229
The 10 Deadliest stampedes/panics 230
The 10 Deadliest structural collapses 231
The 10 Most devastating structural fires 232
The 10 Worst railroad disasters 233
The 10 Sole survivors of deadliest aviation crashes 234

...And Then Pirates Attack 236
The 10 Most recent pirates in US history 236

Sport (general) 238

Top 10 Most dangerous sports in the USA 238

The 10 Inexplicable sports nicknames 239

Top 10 Largest athletes' hearts 240

The 10 Top female badminton players in 2012 241

The 10 Top male badminton players in 2012 242

Top 10 World's largest running events 243

Top 10 Most appearances in a WWE royal rumble 244

The 10 Greatest sports movies 245

Football 245

The 10 Top fantasy football performances ever 246

Top 10 Quarterbacks with the most passing 247

Top 10 Best single-game passing yardage 248

The 10 Most recently defunct NFL teams 249

Top 10 NFL career sacks leaders 250

Top 10 NFL single-season sacks leaders 251

Top 10 NFL career interceptions leaders 252

Top 10 NFL single-season interceptions leaders 253

Top 10 NCAA coaches with the highest win-loss percentage 254

Top 10 Colleges with most Heisman Trophy winners 255

Top 10 Inaugural lingerie football league teams 256

The 10 Best video game athletes 257

Top 10 Teams with most Super Bowl wins 258

Baseball 259

Top 10 Most home runs in a single year 259

Top 10 Best lifetime batting averages 260

Top 10 Best single-season batting averages 261

Top 10 All-time best earned run averages 262

Top 10 Most MLB all-star game appearances 263

Top 10 Best single-season earned run averages 264

Top 10 Teams with the most world series wins 265

Basketball 266
Top 10 Teams winning the most NBA championships 266
Top 10 Unbreakable Wilt Chamberlain records 267
Top 10 Shortest players in NBA history 268

Hockey 269
The 10 Most recently defunct NHL teams 269
Top 10 Teams with most Stanley Cup wins 270

Tennis 271
Top 10 Women with most grand slam titles 271
Top 10 Men with most grand slam titles 272

Golf 273
Top 10 Men with most wins in the PGA majors 273
Top 10 Players with the biggest margins of victory 274
Top 10 Women with most wins in the LPGA majors 275
The 10 Reasons golf is losing popularity 276
Top 10 Most titles won on a PGA tour 277

Olympics & Athletes 278
Top 10 Teams with fewest medals in the summer Olympics 278
The 10 Most frequent winter Olympic entrants to have won no medals 279
Top 10 Nations winning most medals in the summer Olympics 280
Top 10 Nations winning most medals in the winter Olympics 281
Top 10 Nations with most wins in the summer Paralympics 282
Top 10 Most decorated Olympians 283
Top 10 Multi-sport athletes 284

Sources 286
Acknowledgments 288

INTRODUCTION

Our lives are a torrent of trivia. We live in an age when we receive more data from the world in a day than we used to in a month. Much of it is unimportant, but some choice morsels float our way via that river of information: conversation-starters, surprising lessons, and even a few facts you'll never use in a practical sense but that make you ponder your own existence (see Oldest People Who Lived in Three Centuries, page 212).

So how trivial is it, really? If it can impress at a party, teach you something counterintuitive, and expand your philosophical horizons, why ... that's not trifling information. That's the very reason for expanding one's knowledge! The only problem is that aquiring knowledge is addictive—once you start, you need more and more!

That's when it's important to slow down and savor the learning process. To that end, we've tried to include a few silly lists that you'll probably never use (like Bizarre Small-town Slogans, page 179)—as well as some not-so-silly ones you may use if you're prone to grim discussions about the Deadliest Coal Mine Disasters (page 226).

As this book is aimed at men—we sat down and asked ourselves, "What are the things that men want to know, and how can we distill them to their fundamentals?" Unfortunately, there are no records of The 10 Deadliest Ways a Ninja Can Kill You Without Touching You or The First 10 Chimpanzees Who Smoked, so those lists were terminated before they even got started. Instead, we decided to give you an updated account of the world around you, from the types of atoms in your body to the biggest stars in space. We think you'll agree that these are among the cooler subjects to know a thing or two about.

It's good to have a few essential perspectives on the world clarified, and even nicer to have them pared down to a few short names and numbers. After all, you're a busy man with places to go and people to impress. And if one of them should happen to be a tyrannical maniac with a nuclear bomb... well, at least you'll be informed as to its blast radius. (Sadly, not on how to disarm it. We didn't want to research anything that would put us on any FBI watch lists.)

We have tried to show you both micro and macro, by listing everything from the Smartest Animals (page 24) to the Most Populated Countries (page 151), which clearly aren't using many contraceptives! Along the way, you'll learn about birth, marriage, death, disasters and crime.

Sports, of course, are manifest—whether you're a newbie trying to figure out who are the Teams with Most Stanley Cup Wins (page 270), or an experienced fan who wants to knock out that other guy for not understanding how hockey works. We've compiled sports records and trivia lists from the basic to the obscure.

So there you have it: a complete guide to conquering the world in around 250 lists. We've looked at some of the big trends on the Internet itself. After all, the internet is where many of us spend most of our time so it's only right to track how we're using it.

When we were asked to contribute this installment to the late Russell Ash's wonderful series, we started soaking up his previous works. Russell's passion for facts and figures was evident, and we have strived to emulate the quality of his work, which gave the world volumes of fun and authoritative lists. And thanks to you, the reader, for picking up this book. We hope you enjoy it as much as we enjoyed researching it, chasing down the secret statistics that underlie man's universe.

MOST DIVERSE NATIONS, BY MONKEY

	Country	Number of monkey species*
1	Brazil	104
2	Madagascar	93
3	Colombia	39
4	Peru	35
5	Uganda	22
6	Vietnam	19
7	India	17
8	Bangladesh	10
8=	Cambodia	10
10	Suriname	8

*Not counting subspecies
Source: IUCN/SSC Primate Specialist Group

"EXTINCT" ANIMALS THAT WERE LATER REDISCOVERED

	Animal	Rediscovered	Last seen	Interval
1	Coelacanth	1938	Late Cretaceous era	-65 million years
2	Laotian Rock Rat	1996	11 million years ago	approx. 11 million years
3	La Palma Giant Lizard	2007	Around 1500	500 years
4	Bermuda Petrel	1951	1620	331 years
5	Large-Billed Reed-Warbler	2006	1867	139 years
6	New Caledonian Crested Gecko	1994	1866	128 years
7	New Holland Mouse	1967	1843	124 years
8	Cuban Solenodon	1974	1890	84 years
9	Lord Howe Island Stick Insect	2001	1930	71 years
10	Takahe	1948	1898	50 years

TOP 10
DEADLIEST MAN-EATERS

	Name/creature*	Region	Kills
1	Lions of Njombe	Tanzania	1500–2000
2	Champawat Tiger	Nepal/Northern India	436
3	Leopard of Panar	Northern India	400
4	Gustave the Crocodile	Burundi	200‡
5	Leopard of the Central Provinces	Central Provinces of India	150
6	Tsavo maneaters (lions)	Kenya	135•
7	Leopard of Rudraprayag	India	125‡
8	Beast of Gévaudan (likely wolves)	France	113
9	Tigers of Chowgarh	India	50‡
10	Leopard of Gummalapur	India	42

*This list includes animals working together—in the case of the Njombe lion pride, over three generations.
‡Confirmed kills
•Possibly as few victims as 35—studies of hair samples offer evidence for both numbers.

TALLEST BIRDS

	Animal	Average total length
1	Ostrich	6ft 11 in (210 cm)
2	Dalmatian Pelican	5 ft 7 in (170 cm)
3	Southern Cassowary	5 ft 1 in (155 cm)
4	Emu	5 ft in (153 cm)
5	Northern Cassowary	4 ft 11in (149 cm)
6	Greater Rhea	4 ft 5 in (134 cm)
7	Emperor Penguin	3 ft 9 in (114 cm)
8	Dwarf Cassowary	3 ft 5 in (105 cm)
9	Lesser Rhea	3 ft 2 in (96 cm)
10	King Penguin	3 ft (92 cm)

LARGEST CATS*

	Cat	Size
1	Siberian Tiger	931 lb (422 kg)
2	Lion	598 lb (271 kg)
3	Jaguar	299 lb (136 kg)
4	Cougar	264 lb (120 kg)
5	Snow Leopard	165 lb (75 kg)
6	Leopard	143 lb (65 kg)
7	Cheetah	119 lb (54 kg)
8	Eurasian Lynx	79 lb (36 kg)
9	Clouded Leopard	51 lb (23 kg)
10	Caracal	42 lb (19 kg)

*There are eight recognized subspecies of tigers, but this list refers only to the Siberian Tiger—the largest of the eight. Tigers range in weight from 200–931 lb (91–422 kg).
Source: University of Michigan Museum of Zoology

HEAVIEST LIVING REPTILES

	Reptile	Average mass
1	Saltwater Crocodile	1,000 lb (454 kg)
2	Nile Crocodile	840 lb (382 kg)
3	Leatherback Sea Turtle	800 lb (364 kg)
4	Black Caiman	660 lb (300 kg)
5	Orinoco Crocodile	640 lb (290 kg)
6	American Crocodile	610 lb (277 kg)
7	American Alligator	570 lb (260 kg)
8	Aldabra Giant Tortoise	450 lb (205 kg)
9	Gharial	440 lb (200 kg)
10	Galapagos Tortoise	390 lb (175 kg)

GHASTLY WAR ANIMALS

1 Cyborg sharks

DARPA (Defense Advanced Research Projects Agency) buried electrodes in shark brains to steer them remotely, in the hope of following vessels undetected. It also sought to take advantage of the fish's senses to detect human activity at sea.

2 Feinting cows

Trapped in a valley by Roman forces during the Second Punic War, Hannibal Barca tied torches to cows' horns. His Carthaginian army then herded the panicked animals toward a pass guarded by a Roman garrison. His opponent, the general Quintus Fabius Maximus, recognized it for a trick, knowing Hannibal would never try such a blatant assault as to give his army torches and march toward the weakest point. He refused to react to Hannibal's ruse. However, this was exactly the reaction Hannibal expected, and his special forces slaughtered the garrison amid the stampede, clearing an exit for the Carthaginians.

3 War elephants

Although elephants are notoriously difficult to handle, Hannibal (among many others) used them as living tanks to great effect. Ultimately, however, they were his undoing, as the Romans developed a counter-strategy at the Battle of Zama to clear them out of their path, by blasting horns that turned the panicked animals back on Carthaginian forces. Elephants were used in World War II by both sides, to transport materials and to perform certain tasks beyond the reach of machines.

4 Terror camels

Facing 120 war elephants with poisoned tusks and chain-mail armor, the Turkish warlord Timur loaded his camels up with sticks and hay, then set them on fire, prodding them with iron. The screaming animals ran toward the charging elephants, who were completely unnerved and fled, causing havoc among their own army.

5 **Demoralizing pigs**
According to Pliny the Elder, the squealing of pigs was equally unnerving to elephants and would have a similar effect to Timur's terror camels (with less cruelty).

6 **Anti-tank dogs**
In World War II the Soviets trained dogs bearing explosives to approach enemy tanks. The idea was to deposit timed explosives, but a need for greater accuracy led to impact-triggers that also killed the dog. At the same time, the USA worked on something similar for stationary targets but never deployed them.

7 **Incendiary monkeys**
Ancient Chinese soldiers covered monkeys in straw, dipped them in oil, and set them on fire as they were let loose in the enemy's camp. Running around in agony, the poor creatures managed to set tents on fire and cause disarray.

8 **Bat bombs**
Project X-Ray was intended to release parachuted canisters containing hibernating bats. The plan was for the bats to wake up and resume their normal activities across Japan, where many buildings were made of extremely flammable materials. Timed napalm devices attached to the bats would go off simultaneously as they roosted, setting thousands of buildings on fire. This could have potentially caused thousands of conflagrations, but the program completed too late in the war to see any use.

9 **Spy cats**
The CIA got up to some weird stuff in the 1960s, not least of which was the attempt to implant listening devices in a cat, and an antenna in its tail. Their one field test ended immediately, as the poor kitty was run over before it could approach its target. The least believable part of this story, of course, is that anyone could train a cat to go where it's told.

10 **Turkey expediters**
The Nationalists in the Spanish Civil War attached fragile supplies to turkeys, who would descend gently to earth in besieged areas and double as a meal for their recipients.

LONGEST-LIVING ANIMALS

	Animal	Lifespan
1	*Turritopsis nutricula* (a species of jellyfish)	Potentially immortal*
2	Antarctic Sponge	Up to 1,550 years
3	Ocean Quahog (a species of clam)	400+ years
4	Tortoise	Up to 250 years
5	Koi	Up to 226 years
6	Bowhead Whale	Up to 211 years‡
7	Red Sea Urchin	200+ years
8	Lamellibrachia Tube Worm	170–250+ years
9	Tuatara	100–200 years•
10	Geoduck (large saltwater clam)	160+ years

*It can cycle from maturity to childhood and back again, bypassing death.

‡Some living bowhead whales have been found with ivory spears in their body from 200 years ago.

•Descended from an order that lived 200 million years ago

FASTEST MAMMALS

	Animal	Highest recorded speed
1	Pronghorn	80 mph (130 kph)
2	Cheetah	75 mph (121 kph
3	Springbok	71 mph (114 kph)
4	Thomson's Gazelle	58.5 mph (94 kph)
5	Wildebeest	56 mph (90 kph)
6	Greyhound	55 mph (89 kph)
7	Horse	54 mph (87 kph)
8=	Zebra	50 mph (80 kph)
8=	European Hare	50 mph (80 kph)
8=	Lion	50 mph (80 kph)

SMARTEST ANIMALS

	Animal	Notes
1	Chimpanzee	Can use tools, hunt in a pack, learn sign language, and use/combine symbols to communicate complicated ideas.
2	Dolphin	Can use tools, train its children, learn commands, and communicate in a "language" that humans are just starting to decipher.
3	Orangutan	Have a strong culture, featuring strong social bonds and complex methods of communication. Can use tools.
4	Elephant	Cleans its food before consumption, uses tools, can learn commands, and shows empathy toward other elephants.
5	Crow	Will leave nuts in the path of traffic, wait for a light to change, and then collect the nuts afterward.

6	Pig	Is as trainable as a cat or a dog, but can adapt to any environment worldwide, usually outcompeting native species.
7	Squirrel	Not only does it memorize all its hiding spots for food, but it will create false hiding spots to deter thieves.
8	Pigeon	Can remember images even after years of not seeing them. Can also recognize itself in the mirror.
9	Octopus	Can unscrew jars, play games, and navigate through mazes, and possesses a good short-term memory.
10	Rat	Has a remarkable sense of navigation, and can usually find shortcuts through mazes.

Source: Animal Planet

MOST VENOMOUS REPTILES AND AMPHIBIANS

	Creature*	Toxin	Fatal amount (mg)#
1	Indian cobra	Peak V	0.009
2	Mamba	Toxin 1	0.02
3	Brown snake	Texilotoxin	0.05
4=	Inland taipan	Paradotoxin	0.10
=	Mamba	Dendrotoxin	0.10
6	Taipan	Taipoxin	0.11
7=	Indian cobra	Peak X	0.12
=	Poison arrow frog	Batrachotoxin	0.12
9	Indian cobra	Peak 1X	0.17
10	Krait	Bungarotoxin	0.50

*Excluding bacteria
#Quantity required to kill an average-sized human adult
The venom of these creatures is almost unbelievably powerful: 1 milligram (the approximate weight of a banknote) of Mamba Toxin 1 would be sufficient to kill 50 people. Other than reptiles, such creatures as scorpions (0.5 mg) and Black widow spiders (1.0 mg) fall just outside the Top 10. Were bacteria included, 12 kilos of the deadly Botulinus Toxin A (fatal dose just 0.000002 mg) would easily kill the entire population of the world. Even deadly poisons such as strychnine (35 mg), and cyanide (700 mg), seem relatively innocuous in comparison.

THE 10
CUTEST ANIMALS
ON THE PLANET

	Animal	Native to	Resembles
1	Quokka	Western Australia	A smiling micro-kangaroo
2	Chinchilla	Andes montains	A mousy Pikachu
3	Red Panda	Himalayas/China	Laughing cat-raccoon
4	Otter	Worldwide	A curious missile
5	Sugar Glider	Northeastern Australia	Mouse-bat in formal wear
6	Ray	Worldwide	A jolly spaceship
7	Hedgehog	Eastern hemisphere	An emotional pincushion
8	Sloth	Central/South America	Abe Vigoda
9	Ring-tailed cat	Southwest USA/Mexico	Startled cat-raccoon
10	Rabbit	Almost worldwide	The prototypical cute critter

It would be a sad and limited man who denied the adorability of certain animals.
Let our manliness never prevent us from wanting these pets ... even if we say it's only
for our girlfriend.

LONGEST DINOSAURS

	Dinosaur	Length
1	*Amphicoelias fragillimus*	130–200 ft (40–60 m)
2	*Argentinosaurus huinculensis*	98–118 ft (30–36 m)
3	*Supersaurus vivianae*	108–112 ft (33–34 m)
4=	*Sauroposeidon proteles*	92–112 ft (28–34 m)
4=	*Futalognkosaurus dukei*	92–112 ft (28–34 m)
6	*Diplodocus hallorum*	98–109.9 ft (30–33.5m)
7	*"Antarctosaurus" giganteus*	108 ft (33m)
8	*Paralititan stromeri*	85–105 ft (26–32 m)
9=	*Turiasaurus riodevensis*	98 ft (30 m)
9=	*Puertasaurus reuili*	98 ft (30 m)

SHORTEST NON-AVIALAN* DINOSAURS

	Dinosaur	Length
1=	*Parvicursor remotus*	12 in (30 cm)
1=	*"Ornithomimus" minutus*	12 in (30 cm)
1=	*Palaeopteryx thomsoni*	12 in (30 cm)
1=	*Nqwebasaurus thwazi*	12 in (30 cm)
5	*Anchiornis huxleyi*	13 in (34 cm)
6=	*Archaeopteryx lithographica*	16 in (40 cm)
6=	*Xiaotingia zhengi*	16 in (40 cm)
8	*Wellnhoferia grandis*	18 in (45 cm)
9=	*Xixianykus zhangi*	20 in (50 cm)
9=	*Alwalkeria maleriensis*	20 in (50 cm)

*Non-avialan dinosaurs are dinosaurs that do not have feathered wings used for flight.

TOP 10
HYBRID ANIMALS

1   Mule/hinny

Historically one of the most common hybrid animals. As is often the case when two species are capable of mixing genes, its offspring are usually incapable of further reproduction. The horse may be the beast that tamed the West, but it was the mule that made settling possible. It has the stamina of a donkey but a personality that is not so abrasive. Nevertheless, "stubborn as a mule" is a popular saying for a reason.

2   Liger/tiglon

The term for a hybrid sometimes depends on which species is the mother, and the product will be very affected by its parental configuration. In the case of a liger (lion father/tigress mother), it will be much larger even than tigers, which are the largest felid species. Panthera hybrids (some combination of lion, tiger, leopard, or jaguar) are rare because of territorial discretion, but are well documented.

3   Wholphin

A false killer whale (actually a type of dolphin) father and a bottlenose dolphin mother produced the kekaimalu, a fertile(!) wholphin in captivity, which has reproduced twice with a bottlenose dolphin. Some have reportedly been observed in the wild.

4   Polar bear/grizzly hybrid

Some evidence suggests these pairings are on the rise because of global warming. Grizzlies have been spotted in what had been exclusively or primarily polar bear territory. The name for this beast has yet to take— though the Inuit portmanteau of *nanuluk* has a nice ring to it.

5   Beefalo

Is there a tastier name in all the animal kingdom than this pairing of a buffalo and a cow? It is fertile and is actually the result of breeding over multiple generations down to a 37.5 percent bison parentage. Any higher proportion than that and it is officially called a "bison hybrid" although the historical term is "cattalo."

6   ## Cama

In 1998 the first dromedary father/llama mother were interbred by artificial insemination at the—no joke—Camel Reproduction Center in Dubai. Six of these creatures now exist. They have all the power of camels, combined with the wool and the reduced tendency to spit at you that you get in your better class of llama.

7   ## Sheep/goat hybrid

These are much rarer than you'd expect, since there's a big span of six chromosomes between sheep and goats; most of their offspring are stillborn. Botswana successfully produced these hybrids in 2000. The Botswana Ministry of Agriculture named the hybrid class "Toast"—that's the cutest name on this list!

8   ## Killer bees

Warwick Kerr was trying to do a nice thing for humanity by breeding hardier bees that could produce greater quantities of honey for longer stretches of the year. Instead he got a bunch of S.O.Bees. Unfortunately they were accidentally released, which led to further hybridization. They're ridiculously defensive even when they don't need to be.

9   ## Saltwater/Siamese crocodile

What do you get when you combine the massive saltwater croc (up to 20 ft/6 m long!) with the much smaller (about 4 ft/1.2 m long) Siamese croc? Basically, a saltwater crocodile, except that maybe it's fine with freshwater, too. This is a smart strategy by the Siamese to expand their territory, increase their bulk, and rebuild their dwindling numbers.

10 ## Mulard duck

The Muscovy duck has beautiful plumage, but a pox-ugly face. It finds itself a catch of a wife in the adorable Pekin duck, or Long Island duck, as it's also known. It is America's tastiest duck, and that's where their cute offspring the Mulard finds its sociological niche. Since you can force-feed these ducks much easier than you can, say, geese, 35 million Mulards populate France. That's 5.36 ducks for every person in France!

SABER-TOOTHED CREATURES

	Animal	Notes
1	Burrowing Asp	Snake, still alive. Can rotate its teeth to stab sideways.
2	Kaprosuchus	Crocodile-like creature with three sets of saber teeth.
3	Thylacosmilus	A marsupial, similar to a koala or a kangaroo.
4	Smilodon	The famous "saber-toothed tiger."
5	Nimravid	A particularly dangerous cat that frequently attacked and killed each other.
6	Barbourofelis	Looked like a cross between a bear and a saber-toothed tiger. Stronger than a lion.
7	Dinofelis	Jaguar-sized cat that specialized in hunting primates.
8	Gorgonopsid	Displayed both reptilian and mammalian traits, and seen by many as a "link."
9	Uintathere	Vegetarian hippo-like creature. The male used its saber teeth to fight for dominance.
10	Machaeroides	A coyote-sized creature whose teeth helped it fell much larger creatures.

Source: Listverse

FIRST PLAYBOY
PLAYMATES OF THE YEAR

	Year	Playmate
1	1960	Ellen Stratton
2	1961	Linda Gamble
3	1962	Christa Speck
4	1963	June Cochran
5	1964	Donna Michelle
6	1965	Jo Collins
7	1966	Allison Parks
8	1967	Lisa Baker
9	1968	Angela Dorian
10	1969	Connie Kreski

THE 10
MOST RECENT PLAYMATES OF THE YEAR

	Year	Playmate
1	2012	Jaclyn Swedberg
2	2011	Claire Sinclair
3	2010	Hope Dworaczyk
4	2009	Ida Ljungqvist
5	2008	Jayde Nicole
6	2007	Sara Jean Underwood
7	2006	Kara Monaco
8	2005	Tiffany Fallon
9	2004	Carmella DeCesare
10	2003	Christina Santiago

HIGHEST-GROSSING NC-17 FILMS*

	Film	Earnings	Year of release
1	*Showgirls*	$20,350,754	1995
2	*Henry & June*	$11,567,449	1990
3	*The Cook, The Thief, His Wife & Her Lover*	$7,724,701	1990
4	*Bad Education*	$5,211,842	2004
5	*Lust, Caution*	$4,604,982	2007
6	*Tie Me Up! Tie Me Down!*	$4,087,361	1990
7	*Shame*	$3,909,002	2011
8	*The Dreamers*	$2,532,228	2004
9	*Crash*	$2,038,450	1996
10	*Bad Lieutenant*	$2,000,022	1992

*NC-17 stands for "No children under 17 admitted."
Source: Box Office Mojo

THE 10

MOST RECENT AVN* FEMALE PERFORMERS OF THE YEAR

	Performer	Year of award
1	Bobbi Starr	2012
2	Tori Black	2011
3	Tori Black	2010
4	Jenna Haze	2009
5	Sasha Grey	2008
6	Hillary Scott	2007
7	Audrey Hollander	2006
8	Lauren Phoenix	2005
9	Ashley Blue	2004
10	Aurora Snow	2003

*Adult Video News
Source: Information courtesy of The Internet Movie Database (http://www.imdb.com).
Used with permission.

MOST RECENT AVN* MALE PERFORMERS OF THE YEAR

	Performer	Year of award
1	Manuel Ferrara	2012
2	Evan Stone	2011
3	Manuel Ferrara	2010
4	James Deen	2009
5	Evan Stone	2008
6	Tommy Gunn	2007
7	Manuel Ferrara	2006
8	Manuel Ferrara	2005
9	Michael Stefano	2004
10	Lexington Steele	2003

*Adult Video News
Source: Information courtesy of The Internet Movie Database (http://www.imdb.com).
Used with permission.

NATIONS WITH THE BIGGEST POPULATION GROWTH

	Nation	% Growth
1	Qatar	4.93
2	Zimbabwe	4.36
3	Niger	3.36
4	Uganda	3.30
5	Turks and Caicos Islands	3.17
6	Gaza Strip	3.11
7	Burundi	3.10
8	Burkina Faso	3.07
9	United Arab Emirates	3.06
10	Western Sahara	3.03

Source: CIA World Factbook

THE 10
WEIRDEST
CONDOM FLAVORS

1   Gravy-dipped
Not exactly gravy-flavored, but condoms dipped in real gravy and sent to a blogger as promotion for the low budget comedy horror, Thankskilling.

2   Devil
Impressively hand-painted, this condom line produced by Wacky Rubbers included a caricaturesque devil, horns and all. A work of art, but still: yikes.

3   Beer mug
Though Wacky Rubbers closed down, their remaining inventory is being sold off at Willy Wardrobe.

4   Spray-On
Developed with the noble intention of a perfect fit, this conceptual condom never made it past testing, taking two minutes to dry.

5   Vegan Organic Licorice Flavor
In order to avoid using any animal products, vegans have their own line of Glyde prophylactics

6   Tortoise Shells
Pliable, leathery shell contraceptives from this 19th century Japan. Ouch.

7   Ram horns
Okay, that...that's worse. 19th Century Japan again.

8   Intestines
Admittedly less painful than ram horn, but you know what resides in the intestines, don't you?

9   Scotch Flavor
God bless McCondom for devising a new way to combine sex and whisky.

10 Durian
One man's meat is another man's poison, which is never more true when bedecking your undercarriage with the funky odor of this Asian fruit.

EARLY ADULT VIDEO GAMES

1   "Softporn Adventures" (1981)

This game featured a luckless fellow collecting inventory items that would help him seduce beautiful women. Of course, you could say that's more or less the plot of 50 percent of these games, but this one was the first, so it's got a fair claim on that as a synopsis rather than a concept.

2=   "Night Life" (1982)

The first game to feature sexually explicit graphics, Night Life wasn't, wholly speaking, a game, since some of its features were a period-tracking schedule, and a list of useful sexual positions. It was more atmospheric than narrative. Nevertheless, it represented a huge moment in video-game eroticism by depicting sex.

2=   "Seduction of the Condominium Wife" (1982)

Koei, the same publishers as Night Life, made this role-playing adventure game. The objective was, naturally, to seduce the condominium wife.

4=   "Beat 'Em & Eat 'Em" (1982)

Mystique was an early erotic-games publisher, and the first to draw criticism for its crass gameplay. In this game, players control a pair of nude women and attempt, with their mouths, to intercept falling matter from a man atop a building. The game was later revised with a gender-reversed version.

4=   "Custer's Revenge" (1982)

Another Mystique title, in which a nude and erect General Custer attempts to cross the desert under a hail of arrows to reach a nude, bound woman. The game received intense criticism for its disrespectful attitude towards women and Native Americans. Depicting a rape (a charge contested by its designer) and racial strife, the game was revised by another studio to make the female character a willing participant, as well as a playable character attempting to reach Custer.

4= "Bachelor Party" (1982)

The last of the Mystique titles. Essentially a version of the game *Breakout*, but with the player controlling a party drug that restores a nude man's erect state every time he caroms into a nude woman and bounces back to the bottle of the drug. This, too, was retooled (pun intended) for a gender-equal version. These revisions were done by Playaround, which purchased the rights to Mystique's games.

7= "Cathouse Blues"/"Gigolo" (1983)

The player prowls a neighborhood, dodging police and a mugger, in search of a brothel where he/she can have sex. Playaround also released "Burning Desire"/"Jungle Fever" at around this time, which was fairly similar to "Beat 'Em & Eat 'Em."

7= "X-Man" (1983)

A nude man must navigate a maze while avoiding three very Freudian hazards: scissors, crabs, and teeth. If he reaches the door in the middle uncastrated, he is rewarded with sex from a woman. One of the authors had the in-no-way-possible real name of H.K. Poon.

9 "Sex Games" (1985)

This extremely simplistic game required the player to rhythmically waggle the joystick to max out the lust gauge before the potency gauge depleted.

10 "Leisure Suit Larry in the Land of the Lounge Lizards" (1987)

The original 40-year-old virgin, Larry Laffer is perhaps the most mainstream adult-video-game character of the medium, and certainly of its first 20 years. Much of the game was lifted from "Softporn Adventures" (the titles had the same publisher, Sierra On-Line). Having sold a quarter of a million copies, with an estimated 1.5 million further copies pirated, it's one of the most successful video games of all time.

US STATES WITH HIGHEST HIV INFECTION RATE PER CAPITA

	State	Number of AIDS diagnoses in 2010
1	California	4,243
2	New York	4,018
3	Florida	3,658
4	Texas	2,745
5	Illinois	1,364
6	New Jersey	1,352
7	Maryland	1,259
8	Pennsylvania	1,074
9	North Carolina	979
10	Georgia	955

Source: Centers for Disease Control and Prevention

SPECIES WITH LARGEST (ERECT) PENIS

	Species	Average ratio of penis to body size
1	Acorn Barnacle	40 to 1
2	Argentine Blue-bill Duck	2 to 1
3	Banana Slug	1 to 1
4	Greater Hooked Squid	1 to 1
5	Flea	1 to 3
6	Tapir	1 to 4
7	African Elephant	1 to 4
8	*Colymbosathon ecplecticos**	1 to 5
9	Blue Whale	1 to 10
10	Human	1 to 12

*A 425-million-year-old fossil crustacean, the name of which means "swimmer with a large penis."

LONGEST-RUNNING TV SHOWS

	Show	Episodes
1	*Gunsmoke*	635
2	*Lassie*	588
3	*The Simpsons*	508*
4	*Law and Order*	456
5	*Death Valley Days*	451
6	*The Adventures of Ozzie and Harriet*	435
7	*Bonanza*	430
8	*My Three Sons*	380
9	*Dallas*	357
10	*Knots Landing*	344

LONGEST-RUNNING FIRST-RUN SYNDICATED TV SHOWS

	Series	No. of seasons	First broadcast	Last broadcast
1	*The 700 Club*	38	1972	present
2	*Soul Train*	35	1971	2006
3	*America's Black Forum*	33	1977	present
4	*NFL Films Presents*	29	1968	1997
5	*At the Movies*	29	1981	present
6	*Entertainment Tonight*	29	1981	present
7	*MotorWeek*	28	1982	present
8	*The McLaughlin Group*	28	1982	present
9	*Wheel of Fortune*	27	1983	present
10	*Donahue*	27	1969	1996

FILMS WITH THE WORST OPENING WEEKENDS

	Film	Opening*
1	*Hoot*	$3,368,197
2	*The Seeker: The Dark Is Rising*	$3,745,315
3	*Fun Size*	$4,101,017
4	*Meet Dave*	$5,251,918
5	*What's Your Number?*	$5,421,669
6	*Imagine That*	$5,503,519
7	*New York Minute*	$5,962,106
8	*The Wild Thornberrys*	$6,013,847
9	*Quest for Camelot*	$6,041,602
10	*Shorts*	$6,410,339

*Opening refers to the weekend the film had its wide release date (at over 600 theaters).
Source: Box Office Mojo

BIGGEST FILM-OPENING WEEKENDS

	Film	Worldwide opening weekend	Year
1	*Harry Potter and the Deathly Hallows Part 2*	$483,200,000	2011
2	*Harry Potter and the Half-Blood Prince*	$394,000,000	2009
3	*Marvel's The Avengers*	$392,500,000	2012
4	*Transformers: Dark of the Moon*	$382,400,000	2011
5	*Spider-Man 3*	$381,700,000	2007
6	*Pirates of the Caribbean: On Stranger Tides*	$350,600,000	2011
7	*Pirates of the Caribbean: At World's End*	$344,000,000	2007
8	*Harry Potter and the Order of the Phoenix*	$332,700,000	2007
9	*Harry Potter and the Deathly Hallows Part 1*	$330,000,000	2010
10	*Star Wars: Episode III - Revenge of the Sith*	$303,900,000	2005

Source: Box Office Mojo

TOP 10
HIGHEST-GROSSING MOVIES THAT WERE NEVER #1

	Film	Highest rank	Gross	Year of release
1	*My Big Fat Greek Wedding*	2	$241,438,208	2002
2	*Alvin and the Chipmunks: The Squeakquel*	3	$219,614,612	2009
3	*Alvin and the Chipmunks*	2	$217,326,974	2007
4	*Sherlock Holmes*	2	$209,028,679	2009
5	*Ice Age: Dawn of the Dinosaurs*	2	$196,573,705	2009
6	*The Day After Tomorrow*	2	$186,740,799	2004
7	*Dances with Wolves*	2	$184,208,848	1990
8	*A Beautiful Mind*	2	$170,742,341	2001
9	*Chicago*	3	$170,687,518	2002
10	*Bridesmaids*	2	$169,106,725	2011

Source: Box Office Mojo

HIGHEST DOMESTIC-GROSSING MOVIES

	Film	Adjusted gross*	Unadjusted gross	Year of release
1	*Gone with the Wind*	$1,620,397,900	$198,676,459	1939
2	*Star Wars*	$1,428,519,200	$460,998,007	1977
3	*The Sound of Music*	$1,142,171,300	$158,671,368	1965
4	*E.T. The Extra-Terrestrial*	$1,137,671,800	$435,110,554	1982
5	*Titanic*	$1,087,949,000	$658,672,302	1997
6	*The Ten Commandments*	$1,050,620,000	$65,500,000	1956
7	*Jaws*	$1,027,192,100	$260,000,000	1975
8	*Doctor Zhivago*	$995,566,400	$111,721,910	1965
9	*The Exorcist*	$887,005,300	$232,906,145	1973
10	*Snow White and the Seven Dwarfs*	$874,180,000	$184,925,486	1937

*Adjusted for inflation as of September 2012
Source: Box Office Mojo

MOST USEFUL BRUCE CAMPBELL ONE-LINERS

1   "If I was gonna kill you, I'd be stepping over your body right now on my way out the door." (Brisco, The Adventures of Brisco County Jr.)

2   "When the time comes to rescue a bunch of rich women trapped in a brewery, you better step up." (Sam Axe, Burn Notice)

3   "Never look too deep into the mind of a lawyer" (Brisco, The Adventures of Brisco County Jr.)

4   "If you ain't got socks, you ain't got much. But if you got 'em, you might as well pull 'em up." (Himself, AV Club interview)

5   "Get old, you can't even cuss someone and have it bother 'em. Everything you do is either worthless or sadly amusing." (Elvis, Bubba-Ho-Tep)

6   "I'm a man, and you're a woman... at least, last time I checked." (Ash, Evil Dead II)

7   "Hail to the King, baby" (Ash, Army of Darkness)

8   "Actors are nothing more than fugitives from reality." (Himself, If Chins Could Talk: Confessions of a B-Movie Actor)

9   "I have to go exploit a friend in the name of an unsanctioned national security operation, and I don't want to be late." (Sam Axe, Burn Notice)

10 "Dig up a bar of soap and a bottle of Jack. And not in that order." ("Bruce Campbell", My Name Is Bruce)

ACTORS IN HIGHEST GROSSING MOVIES

	Actor	Gross*
1	Tom Hanks	$4,071,300,000
2	Eddie Murphy	$3,810,400,000
3	Harrison Ford	$3,561,600,000
4	Samuel L. Jackson	$3,436,300,000
5	Morgan Freeman	$3,403,900,000
6	Tom Cruise	$3,119,800,000
7	Robin Williams	$3,026,600,000
8	Johnny Depp	$2,981,000,000
9	Bruce Willis	$2,928,100,000
10	Michael Caine	$2,822,100,000

*Aggregate gross of films featuring the actor
Source: Box Office Mojo

FILMS WITH MOST OSCARS

	Film	Awards	Nominations
1	*Titanic* (1997)	11	14
2	*Ben Hur* (1959)	11	12
3	*Lord of the Rings: The Return of the King* (2003)	11	11
4	*West Side Story* (1961)	10	11
5	*The English Patient* (1996)	9	12
6=	Gigi (1958)	9	9
6=	*The Last Emperor* (1987)–	9	9
8=	*Gone with the Wind* (1939)	8	13
8=	*From Here to Eternity* (1953)	8	13
10	*Slumdog Millionaire*	8	10

LOWEST-RATED "BEST MOTION PICTURE" OSCAR WINNERS

	Film	Metascore	Year of release	Also released that year
1	*Crash*	68	2005	*Brokeback Mountain*
2	*A Beautiful Mind*	72	2001	*The Lord of the Rings: The Fellowship of the Ring*
3	*Titanic*	74	1997	*L.A. Confidential*
4	*Chicago*	82	2002	*The Pianist*
4	*Forrest Gump*	82	1994	*The Shawshank Redemption*
6=	*American Beauty*	86	1999	*The Insider*
6=	*Million Dollar Baby*	86	2004	*Sideways*
6=	*The Departed*	86	2006	*Little Miss Sunshine*
9	*The English Patient*	87	1996	*Fargo*
10	*Shakespeare in Love*	87	1998	*Saving Private Ryan*

Source: Metacritic
Metacritic.com is a website that aggregates reviews of music albums, games, movies, TV shows, and DVDs. It takes reviews from all over the Internet, obtains a numerical score for each product, and then averages out the total to calculate the product's rating.

MOST PROFITABLE PIXAR FILMS

	Film	Profit from domestic market	Year
1	*Finding Nemo*	$246 million	2003
2	*Toy Story 3*	$215 million*	2010
3	*The Incredibles*	$169 million	2004
4	*Toy Story*	$162 million	1995
5	*Toy Story 2*	$156 million	1999
6	*Monsters Inc.*	$141 million	2001
7	*Cars*	$124 million	2006
8	*Up*	$118 million	2009
9	*Ratatouille*	$56 million	2007
10	*WALL-E*	$44 million	2008

*If domestic gross, instead of profits, were used, *Toy Story 3* would be #1.
Source: Business Insider

HIGHEST-GROSSING SPORTS MOVIES

	Movie	Gross	Release date
1	*The Blind Side*	$255,959,475	Nov. 20, 2009
2	*Rocky IV*	$127,873,716	Nov. 27, 1985
3	*Rocky III*	$125,049,125	May 28, 1982
4	*Seabiscuit*	$120,277,854	July 25, 2003
5	*Rocky*	$117,235,147	Nov. 21, 1976
6	*Remember the Titans*	$115,654,751	Sept. 29, 2000
7	*Million Dollar Baby*	$100,492,203	Dec. 15, 2004
8	*The Fighter*	$93,617,009	Dec. 10, 2010
9	*Rocky II*	$85,182,160	June 15, 1979
10	*Moneyball*	$75,605,492	Sept. 23, 2011

Real Steel, at $85,468,508, is officially listed at #9. However, since robot fighting isn't currently a recognized sport, we took it off the list.
Source: Box Office Mojo

HIGHEST-GROSSING SUPERHERO MOVIES

	Movie	Worldwide gross*	Release date
1	*Marvel's The Avengers*	$621,460,765	May 4, 2012
2	*The Dark Knight*	$533,345,358	July 18, 2008
3	*The Dark Knight Rises*	$438,033,912	July 20, 2012
4	*Spider-Man*	$403,706,375	May 3, 2002
5	*Spider-Man 2*	$373,585,825	June 30, 2004
6	*Spider-Man 3*	$336,530,303	May 4, 2007
7	*Iron Man*	$318,412,101	May 2, 2008
8	*Iron Man 2*	$312,433,331	May 7, 2010
9	*The Incredibles*	$261,441,092	Nov. 5, 2004
10	*The Amazing Spider-Man*	$260,571,241	July 3, 2012

*As of fall 2012
Source: Box Office Mojo

HIGHEST-GROSSING MOVIES RELEASED IN 2012

	Movie	Domestic Gross*	Release date
1	*Marvel's The Avengers*	$623,357,910	May 4, 2012
2	*The Dark Knight Rises*	$448,139,099	July 20, 2012
3	*The Hunger Games*	$408,010,692	Mar. 23, 2012
4	*Skyfall*	$297,025,010	Nov 9, 2012
5	*The Twilight Saga: Breaking Dawn Part 2*	$289,235,462	Nov 16, 2012
6	*The Hobbit: An Unexpected Journey*	$265,146,005	Dec 14, 2012
7	*The Amazing Spider-Man*	$262,030,663	July 3, 2012
8	*Brave*	$237,277,071	June 22, 2012
9	*Ted*	$218,815,487	June 29, 2012
10	*Madagascar 3: Europe's Most Wanted*	$216,391,482	June 8, 2012

*As of 1 Jan 2013
Source: Box Office Mojo

MANLIEST MOVIES

1   *Die Hard*

2   *Godfather*

3   *Gladiator*

4   *True Grit (1969)*

5   *Casino Royale (2006)*

6   *Rocky*

7   *Heat*

8   *Taxi Driver*

9   *Terminator 2*

10   *Lethal Weapon*

LONGEST FILMS EVER MADE

	Title	Runtime (hours)	Year of release
1	*Modern Times Forever* (Stora Enso Building, Helsinki)	240	2011
2	*Cinématon*	175	1978–2012
3	*Beijing 2003*	150	2004
4	*Untitled #125 (Hickory)*	120	2011
5	*Matrjoschka*	95	2006
6	*The Cure for Insomnia*	87	1987
7	*The Longest Most Meaningless Movie in the World*	48	1968
8	**** (*Four Stars*)	25	1967
9=	*24 Hour Psycho*	24	1993
9=	*The Clock*	24	2010

MOST EXPENSIVE MOVIES EVER MADE

	Movie		Cost*
1	*Pirates of the Caribbean: At World's End*	2007	$336 million
2	*Titanic*	1997	$290 million
3	*Spider-Man 3*	2007	$289 million
4	*Tangled*	2010	$277 million
5	*Harry Potter and the Half-Blood Prince*	2009	$271 million
6	*Waterworld*	1995	$262 million
7	*Pirates of the Caribbean: Dead Man's Chest*	2006	$259 million
8	*Avatar*	2009	$257 million
9	*John Carter*	2012	$250 million
10=	*King Kong*	2005	$246 million
10=	*Spider-Man 2*	2004	$246 million

*Adjusted for inflation

FILMS OF THE 1980S

	Film	Year
1	*E.T. The Extra-Terrestrial*	1982
2	*Return of the Jedi**	1983
3	*The Empire Strikes Back***	1980
4	*Indiana Jones and the Last Crusade*	1989
5	*Rain Man‡*	1988
6	*Raiders of the Lost Ark*	1981
7	*Batman*	1989
8	*Back to the Future*	1985
9	*Who Framed Roger Rabbit*	1988
10	*Top Gun*	1986

*Later retitled *Star Wars: Episode VI – Return of the Jedi*
**Later retitled *Star Wars: Episode V – The Empire Strikes Back*
‡Winner of "Best Picture" Academy Award

The 1980s was clearly the decade of the adventure film, with George Lucas and Steven Spielberg continuing to assert their control of Hollywood, carving up the Top 10 between them, variously as director, writer, or producer of no fewer than seven of the Top 10. Each film earned more than $300 million, while cumulatively the 10 highest-earning films of the decade scooped in more than $4.5 billion at the global box office.

E.T. and *Raiders of the Lost Ark* were both nominated, but neither they nor any of the other highearning films of the 1980s won this Oscar. By way of compensation, each made more than $100,000,000 in North American rentals alone, with *E.T.* raking in more than twice this total and over $700,000,000 worldwide.

LONGEST WIKIPEDIA PAGES

	Page	Bytes
1	List of Advanced Dungeons & Dragons 2nd Edition Monsters	394,120
2	List of Fiction Works Made into Feature Films	370,516
3	List of Federal By-Elections in Canada	365,676
4	List of Clashes in the North Caucasus	364,667
5	List of Other Fictional Presidents of the United States of America	360,613
6	List of Best Selling Musical Artists	358,301
7	List of Townlands in County Galway	343,656
8	List of English Words of French Origin	338,663
9	Japan at the 2010 Asian Games	327,603
10	A Glossary of Cue Sports Terms	324,113

MOST POPULAR TWITTER FEEDS

	Account owner	Account name	Followers*
1	Lady Gaga	@ladygaga	27,804,369
2	Justin Bieber	@justinbieber	25,830,123
3	Katy Perry	@katyperry	24,183,596
4	Rihanna	@rihanna	23,480,469
5	Britney Spears	@britneyspears	19,083,490
6	Barack Obama	@BarackObama	18,026,680
7	Shakira	@shakira	17,410,699
8	Taylor Swift	@taylorswift13	16,849,355
9	Kim Kardashian	@KimKardashian	15,579,748
10	YouTube	@YouTube	14,508,107

*As of January 8, 2012
Source: Twitterholic

MOST POPULAR SCIENCE WEBSITES

	Website	Est. unique visitors per month
1	Howstuffworks	12,000,000
2	NOAA (National Oceanic and Atmospheric Administration)	10,000,000
3	Discovery	9,400,000
4	NASA	8,900,000
5	ScienceDirect	4,500,000
6	ScienceDaily	2,400,000
7	Nature	1,800,000
8	Treehugger	1,700,000
9	PopSci	1,400,000
10	ScienceBlogs	1,250,000

Source: Alexa via eBiz MBA

TOP HUMOR WEBSITES*

	Website	Est. unique visitors per month
1	Break	16,000,000
2	Cracked	8,000,000
3	CollegeHumor	7,000,000
4	VideoBash	5,600,000
5	FailBlog	4,400,000
6	TheOnion	4,150,000
7	eBaumsWorld	4,100,000
8	theCHIVE	4,075,000
9	9GAG	4,050,000
10	xkcd	2,200,000

Source: Alexa via eBIZ MBA

THE 10
TOP INTERNET HOAXES

1   ## Bonsai Kittens (2000)
A website promoting the supposedly ancient art of 'kitten bonsai'.

2   ## Bill Gates buys the Catholic Church (1994)
A rumour was spread that Bill Gates had purchased the Catholic Church, having identified religion as a promising market.

3   ## ManBeef.com (2001)
This website, supposedly selling human meat, included convincing colour photography and a host of 'delicious' recipes.

4   ## The Chaos Cloud (2005)
An online article describing the chaos cloud: a mass in outer space eliminating stars and planets in its way, and set to reach Earth in 2014.

5   ## SaveToby.com (2005)
The owner of this site claimed he could not afford to keep his rabbit, and that unless he received $50,000, he would be forced to eat him. After receiving $24,000 and a book deal, he decided not to boil his bunny.

6   ## Snoop Dogg becomes a Mormon (2008)
This story was published on a fake CNN site as an April Fool's Day prank. The rapper was reported to have converted after months studying the faith.

7   ## Mentos and Coke (2006)
A chain email reporting the death of a small boy in Brazil from the combination of Mentos candy and Coke.

8   ## Charging an iPod with an Onion (2007)
A YouTube video seeming to show an iPod being charged using only an onion, a bottle of Gatorade, a screwdriver and a USB cord fooled many.

9   ## The Derbyshire Fairy (2006)
Prop-maker Dan Baines creates a 'fairy corpse' to sell on eBay.

10   ## World Jump Day (2006)
A fake scam to convince 600 million people to jump at the same time in order to influence the Earth's orbit and prevent global warming.

BUSIEST WEBSITES IN THE USA*

1   Google
2   Facebook
3   YouTube
4   Yahoo!
5   Amazon.com
6   Wikipedia
7   eBay
8   Twitter
9   Craigslist
10 Windows Live

*As of October 2012
Source: ©2012 Alexa Internet (www.alexa.com)

THE 10
LESSER-KNOWN WIKIMEDIA PROJECTS

1	Meta-Wiki	Helps plans and coordinate other Wikimedia projects.
2	Wikimedia Commons	Hosts images, sounds, and other media that is free to use.
3	Wikibooks	Specializes in free content textbooks, as well as annotated texts.
4	Wikinews	A free-content news site created through collaborative journalism.
5	Wikiquote	A collection of famous quotations from prominent people, books and more.
6	Wikisource	Provides free content textual sources in a number of different languages.
7	Wikispecies	Aimed at scientists, this is a free content catalogue of all known species.
8	Wikiversity	Offers free courses, tutorials, and more.
9	Wiktionary	A multilingual, free source dictionary.
10	Wikivoyage	Launched in January of 2013, Wikivoyage is Wikimedia's new collaborative travel guide.

THE 10
GREATEST INTERNET APRIL FOOL'S PRANKS OF 2012

1   Google Maps goes 8-Bit:
     The site managed to cover the world in Nintendo homage. Simply
     stunning in scope.

2   AdBlock is now CatBlock:
     AdBlock knows what the internet wants: ads replaced with pictures of cats.

3   The Register claimed Apple had successfully filed for
     patent on the Rectangle:
     The internet screeched in the halls of tomfoolery.

4   Funny or Die leaks Charlize Theron's sex tape:
     It's hard to match this one for the sheer, gasping flare of hope that
     too soon fizzles on the date.

5   Reddit Timeline:
     Delight at Reddit posts from the future—or ones that precede the internet.

6   Tech Radar's Photoshop age filters:
     No, internet, the most intense photo-editing software on Earth is not
     refocusing on the tricks done by goofy phone apps.

7   Google Nigeria:
     The world's phishiest nation got specifically called out by the search giant.

8   YouTube on DVD:
     72 hours of content are uploaded to YouTube every minute, so...no.

9   Gmail Tap:
     Morse code is still more reliable and preferable than the deadly
     touchscreen/autocorrect duo.

10   Toshiba's Spectacle:
     Toshiba claim the world's first 3D monocle.

MOST VIEWED YOUTUBE VIDEOS OF ALL TIME

	Video	Number of views*
1	PSY—"Gangnam Style"	1,146,679,934
2	Justin Bieber ft. Usher—"Baby"	777,874,421
3	Jennifer Lopez ft. Pitbull—"On the Floor"	593,444,394
4	Eminem ft. Rihanna—"Love the Way you Lie"	493,601,686
5	Shakira—"Waka Waka (This Time for Africa)"	491,488,185
6	Lady Gaga—"Bad Romance"	485,463,545
7	LMFAO ft. Lauren Bennett and Goonrock—"Party Rock Anthem"	480,335,194
8	"Charlie Bit My Finger—Again!"	479,028,024
9	Michel Teló—"Ai Se Eu Te Pego"	429,228,136
10	Don Omar ft. Lucenzo—"Danza Kuduro"	384,247,689

*As of fall 2012
Source: YouTube

TOP MUSICIANS WITH SINGLE STAGE NAMES

	Musician	Real Name
1	Bono	Paul David Hewson
2	Cher	Cherilyn Sarkisian
3	Common	Lonnie Rashid Lynn, Jr.
4	Eminem	Marshall Bruce Mathers III
5	Jewel	Jewel Kilcher
6	Ke$ha	Kesha Rose Sebert
7	Ludacris	Christopher Brian Bridges
8	Madonna	Madonna Louise Ciccone
9	Sting	Gordon Matthew Thomas Sumner
10	Timbaland	Timothy Zachery Mosley

FAVORITE BASS SOLOS OF ALL TIME

1   Portrait of Tracy by Jaco Pastorius
Pastorius has an ability on bass guitar in a way we'll probably never hear again.

2   U Can't Hold No Groove... by Victor Wooten
When you listen to this and assume you're hearing three bass parts playing at once—that was all done in one go, by one person and one instrument.

3   My Generation by The Who
Many of the solos on this list feature lightning-fast notes. But chances are this one is the one you know off the top of your head.

4   Maxwell Murder by Rancid
Punk bassists are sometimes maligned for not venturing outside the two lowest strings on their guitars. Not here.

5   (Anesthesia) Pulling Teeth by Metallica
The late Cliff Burton plays something hre you'd never believe was a bass solo.

6   Addicted to That Rush by Mr. Big
Feel free to scoff at this band, but bassist, Billy Sheehan, is widely regarded as perhaps the greatest rock bassist ever.

7   Tommy the Cat by Primus
The entire song is an absolute clinic about how to mistreat your strings.

8   YYZ by Rush
A song peppered with Geddy Lee's signature machine-gun-style notes.

9   The Dance of Eternity [Scene Seven] by Dream Theater
Your stereo is just fine—that rumble is just bass virtuoso John Myung playing so quickly that it almost sounds like a different instrument.

10 Aeroplane by the Red Hot Chili Peppers
A fun, bouncy, methodical end solo that serves as a perfect transition from Aeroplane's verse into its head-bopping outro.

OUR 10
FAVORITE GUITAR SOLOS OF ALL TIME

1   The Star Spangled Banner by Jimi Hendrix
    Hendrix playing this at Woodstock has become an icon, which is
    something that very few songs can claim.

2   Stairway to Heaven by Led Zeppelin
    Jimmy Page might not shine brighter than he does here.

3   Cliffs of Dover by Eric Johnson
    With the opening riff, you know you're in for a virtuoso performance, and
    Eric Johnson delivers.

4   November Rain by Guns 'n Roses
    A great example of why people aged 25–45 worship at the altar of Slash.

5   Killing in the Name by Rage Against the Machine
    Guitarist Tom Morello is well known for making his guitar sound like anything.

6   Whole Lotta Love by Led Zeppelin
    Not only is Jimmy Page's solo an absolute killer, but it's placed perfectly
    within the song.

7   Eruption by Van Halen
    A perfect summary of "that Van Halen sound."

8   Crossroads by Cream
    This signature solo of Eric Clapton is frequently held up as one of the
    pantheon guitar performances of all time.

9   Rain of a Thousand Flames by Rhapsody
    The most absurdly over-the-top song you could ever imagine. The entire
    song is self-indulgent, and the solo is no different.

10 Trippin' On a Hole in a Paper Heart by Stone Temple Pilots
    Call this a personal favorite.

OUR 10

FAVORTE DRUM SOLOS OF ALL TIME

1 Moby Dick by Led Zeppelin
John Bonham's epic drum solo in this song is a well-justified moment in the spotlight.

2 Frankenstein by The Edgar Winter Group
The extended drum solo in the middle is a perfect transition from the song's rocking beginning to its epic end.

3 In-a-gadda-da-vita by Iron Butterfly
Drummer Ron Bushy Bushy makes sure to take up every ounce of time with as many beats humanly as possible in the time afforded.

4 My Generation by The Who
This rapid-fire solo should come as no surprise to anyone.

5 2112 by Rush
Peart plays "lead drums" for much of this song. That alone deserves a nod.

6 Toad by Cream
One must wonder how Ginger Baker's arms were able to hold out for all of Cream's live shows.

7 Hot for Teacher by Van Halen
A technically proficient drum line of all time.

8 Wipeout by The Surfaris
From the opening, drummer Ron Wilson shows why he's worth a paycheck.

9 The End by The Beatles
While this solo doesn't overstretch its place in the song, it's still a perfect setup to the rest of the track.

10 Lie in Our Graves by The Dave Matthews Band
Drummer Carter Beauford makes his performance on this piece the most distinctive part of this track.

BIGGEST-SELLING SINGLES OF ALL TIME

	Artist	Song	Year	Gross
1	Bing Crosby	"White Christmas"	1942	$50 million
2	Elton John	"Candle in the Wind 1997"	1997	$33 million
3	Bing Crosby	"Silent Night"	1935	$30 million
4	Bill Haley & His Comets	"Rock Around the Clock"	1954	$25 million
5	Elvis Presley	"It's Now or Never"	1960	$22 million
6	USA for Africa	"We Are the World"	1985	$20 million
7	The Ink Spots	"If I Didn't Care"	1939	$19 million
8	Baccara	"Yes Sir, I Can Boogie"	1977	$18 million
9	Gene Autry	"Rudolph the Red-Nosed Reindeer"	1949	$18 million
10	Celine Dion	"My Heart Will Go On"	1997	$15 million

TOP-SELLING ALBUMS OF ALL TIME

	Artist	Album	Year of release	No. of times Platinum
1=	Michael Jackson	*Thriller*	1982	29
1=	Eagles	*Their Greatest Hits (1971–1975)*	1976	29
3=	Pink Floyd	*The Wall*	1979	23
3=	Billy Joel	*Greatest Hits Vol. I & II*	1985	23
3=	Led Zeppelin	*IV*	1971	23
6	AC/DC	*Back in Black*	1980	22
7	Garth Brooks	*Double Live*	1998	21
8	Shania Twain	*Come On Over*	1997	20
9=	The Beatles	*The Beatles*	1968	19
9=	Fleetwood Mac	*Rumours*	1977	19

TOP 10

MOST EXPENSIVE GUITARS

	Guitar	Value
1	Reach out to Asia Fender Stratocaster*	$2,700,000
2	A 1968 Stratocaster owned by Jimi Hendrix and played at Woodstock	est. $2,000,000
3	Bob Marley's custom-made Washburn 22 series Hawk	est. $1,200,000–$2,000,000
4	Eric Clapton's Stratocaster hybrid nicknamed "Blackie"	$959,500
5	A 1964 Gibson ES0335 TDC, owned by Eric Clapton	$847,500
6	A C.F. Martin & Co. made around 1939, owned by Eric Clapton	$791,500
7	Stevie Ray Vaughan's 1965 Fender Composite Stratocaster, nicknamed "Lenny"	$623,500
8	A 1964 Gibson SG owned by John Lennon and George Harrison	$570,000
9	Eric Clapton's 23-karat gold Stratocaster	$455,550
10	Leo Fender's 1949 Broadcaster prototype	$375,000

*Signed by Mick Jagger, Keith Richards, Eric Clapton, Brian May, Jimmy Page, David Gilmour, Jeff Beck, Pete Townshend, Mark Knopfler, Ray Davis, Liam Gallagher, Ronnie Wood, Tony Iommi, Angus and Malcolm Young, Paul McCartney, Sting, Ritchie Blackmore, Def Leppard, and Bryan Adams.
Source: My Les Paul

OLDEST WRITTEN LANGUAGES

	Language	First appearance
1	Sumerian	c. 2,900 BC
2	Egyptian	c. 2,700 BC
3=	Akkadian	c. 2,400 BC
3=	Eblaite	c. 2,400 BC
5	Elamite	c. 2,300 BC
6	Hurrian	21st century BC
7=	Luwian	18th century BC
7=	Minoan	18th century BC
9	Hittite	c. 1,650 BC
10	Canaanite	c. 1,500 BC

BIZARRE BOOK TITLES

	Book title	Author
1	*How to Avoid Huge Ships*	John W. Trimmer
2	*Fancy Coffins to Make Yourself*	Dale L. Power
3	*Scouts in Bondage*	Geoffrey Prout
4	*Lightweight Sandwich Construction*	J. M. Davies
5	*Be Bold with Bananas*	Crescent Books
6	*Natural Bust Enlargement with Total Mind Power*	Donald Wilson, M.D.
7	*Bombproof your Horse*	Sgt. Rick Pelicano
8	*Superfluous Hair and its Removal*	A. F. Niemoeller
9	*The Flat-Footed Flies of Europe*	Peter J. Chandler
10	*How to Read a Book*	Mortimer J. Adler and Charles Van Doren

THE 10
TOP PULP CHARACTERS STILL IN PRINT

1. **Tarzan (1912)**
   The man raised by apes had two novels published in 2011 and 2012.

2. **Fu Manchu (1913)**
   The (controversial) criminal genius is still appearing in novels as of 2012.

3. **John Carter of Mars (1917)**
   The Martian warlord is as immortal in our world as he is on his own, appearing in an ultra-expensive film in 2012 that failed to recoup its budget.

4. **Zorro (1919)**
   The Los Angeles avenger chose a different path than his peers, with a 2008 play, a handheld video game, and a couple of audio dramas in 2011.

5. **Buck Rogers (1928)**
   With plans for a comic series in 2013, Buck struggles on nobly after the 2010 demise of his proposed web video series.

6. **Solomon Kane (1928)**
   Badass Puritan Kane slew evil in a 2008 film that only saw US release in 2012, plus three recent comic book miniseries.

7. **The Shadow (1931)**
   The Shadow leapt from the radio in 1930 to pulps, and thrived in both media. In 2012 Dynamite Ent. began publishing his comics.

8. **Conan the Barbarian (1932)**
   Debuting in the last four years of creator Robert E. Howard's life, the Cimmerian warrior has made prolific appearances, including a 2011 film.

9. **Doc Savage (1933)**
   The adventurer-inventor influenced both Superman and Indiana Jones, and recently appeared in DC Comics.

10. **Flash Gordon (1934)**
    This Yale polo player was still overthrowing galactic tyranny in a 2008 TV show and comic books in 2011 and 2012.

BEST-SELLING BOOKS OF THE 21ST CENTURY

	Title	Author	Year of publication	Sales*
1	*Harry Potter and the Deathly Hallows*	J.K. Rowling	2007	8,113,688
2	*Harry Potter and the Half-Blood Prince*	J.K. Rowling	2005	7,450,354
3	*Twilight*	Stephanie Meyer	2006	6,248,401
4	*Fifty Shades of Grey*	E.L. James	2012	6,051,725
5	*Breaking Dawn*	Stephanie Meyer	2008	5,943,870
6	*New Moon*	Stephanie Meyer	2008	5,532,767
7	*The Shack*	William P. Young	2007	5,468,113
8	*Eclipse*	Stephanie Meyer	2007	5,392,088
9	*Eat, Pray, Love: One Woman's Search for Everything*	Elizabeth Gilbert	2007	5,229,835
10	*The Kite Runner*	Khaled Hosseini	2004	5,030,093

*As of October 2012
Source: Nielsen BookScan US

THE 10

MOST RECENT RECIPIENTS OF THE NOBLE PRIZE FOR LITERATURE

	Author	Nation	Year
1	Mo Yan	China	2012
2	Tomas Tranströmer	Sweden	2011
3	Mario Vargas Llosa	Peru	2010
4	Herta Müller	Germany	2009
5	J. M. G. Le Clézio	France	2008
6	Doris Lessing	United Kingdom	2007
7	Orhan Pamuk	Turkey	2006
8	Harold Pinter	United Kingdom	2005
9	Elfriede Jelinek	Austria	2004
10	J. M. Coetzee	South Africa	2003

LONGEST BOOKS EVER WRITTEN

	Book	Author	Words
1	*A la recherche du temps perdu (In Search of Lost Time/ Remembrance of Things Past)*	Marcel Proust	1,200,000
2	*Clarissa, or, the History of a Young Lady*	Samuel Richardson	984,870
3	*Ponniyin Selvan (The Son of Ponni)*	Kalki Krishnamurthy	900,000
4	*Poor Fellow My Country*	Xavier Herbert	852,000
5	*Sironia, Texas*	Madison Cooper	840,000
6	*Romance of the Three Kingdoms*	Luo Guanzhong	800,000
7	*A Suitable Boy*	Vikram Seth	593,674
8	*War and Peace*	Leo Tolstoy	587,287
9	*Atlas Shrugged*	Ayn Rand	565,223
10	*Il mulino del Po (The Mill on the Po)*	Riccardo Bacchelli	559,830

THE 10
MOST RECENT CARNEGIE MEDAL WINNERS

	Year*	Author/title
1	2012	Patrick Ness, *A Monster Calls*
2	2011	Patrick Ness, *Monsters of Men*
3	2010	Neil Gaiman, *The Graveyard Book*
4	2009	Siobhan Dowd, *Bog Child*
5	2008	Philip Reeve, *Here Lies Arthur*
6	2007	Meg Rosoff, *Just in Case*
7	2005	Mal Peet, *Tamar*
8	2004	Frank Cottrell Boyce, *Millions*
9	2003	Jennifer Donnelly, *A Gathering Light*
10	2002	Sharon Creech, *Ruby Holler*

*Prior to 2007, publication year; since 2007, award year—hence there was no 2006 award
Established in 1937, the Carnegie Medal is awarded annually by the Library Association
for an outstanding English-language children's book published during the previous year. It
is named in honor of Scots-born millionaire Andrew Carnegie, who was a notable library
benefactor. In its early years, winners included such distinguished authors as Arthur
Ransome, Noel Streatfeild, Walter de la Mare, and C. S. Lewis, while among notable post-
war winners are books such as *Watership Down* by Richard Adams.

SELDOM-USED ENGLISH PUNCTUATION

Name Symbol

1	Interrobang	‽
2	Exclamation comma	⸮
3	Question comma	?
4	Irony mark*	؟
5	Doubt point	⸮
6	Certitude point	†
7	Acclamation point	⸍
8	Authority point	↑
9	Love point	♡
10	Snark mark	.~

*Also known as percontation point

FASTEST-GROWING MAGAZINE GENRES

	Genre	Number of titles in 2000	Number of titles in 2010	Growth in number of titles
1	Ethnic	419	978	559
2	Travel	669	829	160
3	Regional interest	794	939	145
4	Medicine	959	1,100	141
5	Real estate	190	324	134
6	College alumni	442	569	127
7	Bridal	40	150	110
8	Nursing	130	187	57
9	Golf	98	140	42
10	Senior citizens	105	146	41

Source: Association of Magazine Media

TOP COMIC CREATORS WHO USED PSEUDONYMS

	Pen Name	Real Name
1	Stan Lee	Stanley Martin Lieber
2	Jack Kirby	Jacob Kurtzberg
3	Silas	Winsor McCay
4	Willis Rensie	Will Eisner
5	Moebius	Jean Giraud
6	Eli Katz	Gil Kane
7	Peyo	Pierre Culliford
8	Hergé	Georges Remi
9	Curt Vile	Alan Moore
10	Christopher Priest	James Owley

MOST POPULAR ART EXHIBITIONS IN 2011

	Exhibition/Gallery	Daily visitors*	Total visitors
1	The Magical World of Escher‡ /Centro Cultural Banco do Brasil, Rio de Janeiro	9,677	573,691
2	Kukai's World: the Arts of Esoteric Buddhism/Tokyo National Museum, Tokyo	9,108	550,399
3	Landscape Reunited/National Palace Museum, Taipei	8,828	847,509
4	Alexander McQueen: Savage Beauty/ Metropolitan Museum of Art, New York	8,025	661,509
5	Claude Monet (1840–1926) /Grand Palais, Paris	7,609	913,064
6	Photoquai‡\Musée Quai Branly, Paris	7,304	438,225
7	Mariko Mori: Oneness‡/Centro Cultural Banco do Brasil, Rio de Janeiro	6,991	538,328
8	Monumenta: Anish Kapoor/ Grand Palais, Paris	6,967	277,687
9	Laurie Anderson‡/Centro Cultural Banco do Brasil, Rio de Janeiro	6,934	535,929
10	The Prado Museum at the Hermitage/ State Hermitage Museum, St. Petersburg	6,649	530,000

*Ranked according to the number of visitors per day, not total visitors
‡Free admission
Source: *The Art Newspaper*

MOST EXPENSIVE SCULPTURES EVER SOLD

	Artist/Sculpture/Year sculpted	Date of sale	Sale price
1	Alberto Giacometti/ *L'Homme qui marche I*/1961	Feb. 3, 2010	$104,300,000
2	n/a/*Guennol Lioness*/ c. 3000 BC	Dec. 5, 2007	$57,200,000
3	Alberto Giacometti/ *Grande tête mince*|1955	May 4, 2010	$53,300,000
4	Amedeo Modigliani/*Tête* 1910–1912	June 14, 2010	$52,600,000
5	Henri Matisse/*Nu de dos, 4 état (Back IV)*/1958	Nov. 3, 2010	$48,800,000
6	Constantin Brâncuşi/ *Madame LR (Portrait de Mme LR)*/1914–1917	Feb. 24, 2009	$37,600,000
7	Pablo Picasso/*Tête de femme (Dora Maar)*/1941	Nov. 7, 2007	$29,100,000
8	n/a/*Artemis and the Stag*/ c.100 BC–AD 100	June 7, 2007	$28,600,000
9	Constantin Brâncuşi/ *Bird in Space*/1922–1923	May 5, 2005	$27,500,000
10	Alberto Giacometti/*Grande Femme Debout II*/ 1959–1960	May 6, 2008	$27,400,000

As of November 2011

MOST EXPENSIVE PHOTOGRAPHS EVER SOLD

Photographer/Photograph/ Year photographed	Date of sale	Sale price
1 Andreas Gursky/*Rhein II*/1999	Nov. 8, 2011	$4,338,500
2 Cindy Sherman/*Untitled #96*/1981	May 2011	$3,890,500
3 Jeff Wall/*Dead Troops Talk (A vision after an ambush of a Red Army patrol, near Moqor, Afghanistan, winter 1986)*/1991	May 8, 2012	$3,666,500
4 Andreas Gursky/*99 Cent II Diptychon*/2001	Feb. 2007	$3,346,456
5 Edward Steichen/*The Pond—Moonlight*/1904	Feb. 2006	$2,928,000
6 Cindy Sherman/*Untitled #153*/1985	Nov. 2010	$2,700,000
7 Unknown photographer/*Billy the Kid*/1879–1880	June 2011	$2,300,000
8 Dmitry Medvedev/*Tobolsk Kremlin*/2009	Jan. 2010	$1,750,000
9 Edward Weston/*Nude*/1925	Apr. 2008	$1,609,000
10 Alfred Stieglitz/*Georgia O'Keeffe (Hands)*/1919	Feb. 2006	$1,470,000

MOST EXPENSIVE PAINTINGS EVER SOLD

	Title/Artist	Adjusted sale price*	Unadjusted sale price
1	*The Card Players* by Paul Cézanne	$254,000,000	$250,000,000
2	*No. 5, 1948* by Jackson Pollock	$159,400,000	$140,000,000
3	*Woman III* by Willem de Kooning	$156,500,000	$137,500,000
4	*Portrait of Adele Bloch-Bauer I* by Gustav Klimt	$152,600,000	$135,000,000
5	*Portrait of Dr. Gachet* by Vincent van Gogh	$146,500,000	$82,500,000
6	*Bal du moulin de la Galette* by Pierre-Auguste Renoir	$138,700,000	$78,100,000
7	*Garçon à la pipe* by Pablo Picasso	$126,400,000	$104,200,000
8	*The Scream* by Edvard Munch	$119,900,000	$119,900,000
9	*Nude, Green Leaves and Bust* by Pablo Picasso	$112,000,000	$106,500,000
10	*Portrait of Joseph Roulin* by Vincent Van Gogh	$108,000,000	$58,000,000‡

*Adjusted for inflation as of March 2012
‡Plus exchange of works

BIGGEST VIDEO GAME CONVENTIONS

	Name	Place	Highest attendance
1	Gamescon	Cologne, Germany	275,000
2	TGS (Tokyo Game Show)	Tokyo, Japan	200,000+
3	Igromir	Moscow, Russia	105,000
4	G-Star	South Korea	82,000
5	Pax Prime	Seattle, USA	70,000+
6	Brazil Game Show	Brazil	60,000
7	Pax East	Boston, USA	52,290
8	E3	Los Angeles, USA	45,700
9	Gencon	Indiana, USA	36,733
10	Eurogamer Expo	London, UK	34,500

BEST-SELLING VIDEO GAMES OF ALL TIME

	Game	Units sold	System
1	Wii Sports	41,650,000	Nintendo Wii
2	Super Mario Brothers	40,240,000	NES
3	Pokémon Red, Green, and Blue	31,380,000	Game Boy
4	Tetris	30,260,000	Game Boy
5	Duck Hunt	28,310,000	NES
6	Pokémon Gold and Silver	23,110,000	Game Boy
7	Nintendogs	21,600,000	Nintendo DS
8	Super Mario World	20,610,000	SNES
9	Wii Play	20,300,000	Nintendo Wii
10	New Super Mario Brothers	18,430,000	Nintendo DS

HIGHEST-GROSSING ARCADE GAMES

	Game	Gross earnings*
1	Pac-Man	$7,610,000,000
2	Space Invaders	$7,250,000,000
3	Street Fighter 2	$2,400,000,000
4	Asteroids	$1,300,000,000
5	Defender	$1,200,000,000
6	Mortal Kombat	$718,000,000
7	Donkey Kong	$684,000,000
8	Mushiking: The King of Beetles	$588,130,000
9	Oshare Majo: Love and Berry	$335,880,000
10	Centipede	$193,310,000

*Adjusted for inflation

BEST-SELLING VIDEO GAME CONSOLES OF ALL TIME*

	System	Year	Units sold
1	Sony PlayStation 2	2000	153,600,000
2	Sony PlayStation	1994	102,490,000
3	Nintendo Wii	2006	96,560,000
4	Microsoft Xbox 360	2005	68,300,000
5	Sony PlayStation 3	2006	63,900,000
6	Nintendo Entertainment System	1983	61,910,000
7	Super Nintendo Entertainment System	1990	49,100,000
8	Sega Genesis	1988	40,000,000
9	Nintendo 64	1996	32,930,000
10	Atari 2600	1977	30,000,000

*The sales figure on many of these games are likely to be skewed due to the fact that they were "pack-in games," or, games that came with a system. Wii Sports, Super Mario Brothers, Tetris, Duck Hunt, Nintendogs, Super Mario World, and New Super Mario Brothers were all pack-in games.

BEST-SELLING VIDEO GAME FRANCHISES

	Franchise	Sales
1	Mario	$450,220,000
2	Pokémon	$219,280,000
3	Wii Series	$192,760,000
4	The Sims	$150,000,000
5	Tetris	$125,000,000
6	Grand Theft Auto	$114,000,000
7	Final Fantasy	$102,040,000
8=	Call of Duty	$100,000,000
8=	FIFA	$100,000,000
8=	Need for Speed	$100,000,000

TOP 10
MOST BIZARRE GAMES MERCHANDISE CREATED

	Game/Franchise	Merchandise
1	Super Mario Bros	Power Shower Adaptor
2	Pokémon	Curry
3	Portal	Cookie Jar
4	Street Fighter: The World Warrior	Toy Chopper Bike
5	Final Fantasy	Make-Up Bag
6	Little Big Planet	Espresso Set
7	Minecraft	Necklace
8	Sonic The Hedgehog	Soda Drink
9	Ms. Pac Man	Air Freshener
10	Asteroids	Costume: Dress Up As Asteroids

BEST-SELLING HANDHELD VIDEO GAME SYSTEMS OF ALL TIME

	System	Year	Units sold
1	Nintendo DS	2004	152,050,000
2	Nintendo Game Boy, Game Boy Color	1989,1998	118,690,000 (combined)
3	Nintendo Game Boy Advance	2001	81,510,000
4	Sony PlayStation Portable	2004	75,400,000
5	Nintendo 3DS	2011	19,000,000
6	Sega Game Gear	1990	11,000,000
7	Nokia N-Gage	2003	3,000,000
8	Sony PlayStation Vita	2011	2,200,000
9	SNK Neo Geo Pocket, Neo Geo Pocket Color	1998,1999	2,000,000
10	NEC TurboExpress	1990	1,500,000

MOST POPULAR FREE IPHONE APPS EVER*

1   Facebook

2   Pandora Radio

3   Words with Friends Free

4   Skype

5   The Weather Channel®

6   Google Search

7   Google Earth

8   Angry Birds Free

9   Shazam

10   Netflix

*Apple has not released actual sales figures.

MOST POPULAR PAID-FOR IPHONE APPS EVER*

1. Angry Birds
2. Fruit Ninja
3. Doodle Jump
4. Cut the Rope
5. Angry Birds Seasons
6. Words with Friends
7. Tiny Wings
8. Angry Birds Rio
9. Pocket God
10. Camera+

*Apple has not released actual sales figures.

MOST POPULAR FREE IPAD APPS EVER*

1   Angry Birds HD Free
2   The Weather Channel® for iPad
3   Netflix
4   Skype for iPad
5   Kindle
6   ABC Player
7   Pandora Radio
8   Angry Birds Rio HD Free
9   CNN App for iPad
10 Words with Friends HD Free

*Apple has not released actual sales figures.

MOST POPULAR PAID-FOR IPAD APPS EVER*

1   Pages
2   Angry Birds HD
3   Angry Birds Seasons HD
4   Penultimate
5   Scrabble for iPad
6   Fruit Ninja HD
7   GarageBand
8   GoodReader for iPad
9   Angry Birds Rio HD
10   Cut the Rope HD

*Apple has not released actual sales figures.

BIGGEST MMORPGS*

	Title	Subscribers (100k)‡
1	World of Warcraft (global)	102
2	Aion	20.4
3	Star Wars: The Old Republic	10.5
4	Lineage	10
5	Runescape	8.5
6	Dofus	5.3
7	EVE Online	4.9
8	Final Fantasy XI	3.6
9	Lord of the Rings Online	2.65
10	Rift	2.49

*MMORPG = Massively Multiplayer Online Role Playing Game
‡As of October 15, 2012. This list should be taken with a pinch of salt, as it is based on the most recent data from each developer. In some cases, recent data is pitted against data from a couple of years ago—a lifetime in MMORPGs, where popularity can wax and wane rapidly. Nevertheless, these are the most recently tabulated numbers for all properties.
Source: MMOData.net

TOP AUTOMAKERS WORLDWIDE

	Automaker	Brand value*
1	Toyota	$27,764 million
2	Mercedes Benz	$27,445 million
3	BMW	$24,554 million
4	Honda	$19,431 million
5	Volkswagen	$7,857 million
6	Ford	$7,483 million
7	Audi	$6,171 million
8	Hyundai	$6,005 million
9	Porsche	$4,580 million
10	Nissan	$3,819 million

*Brand value is the perceived worth of the brand itself, not the value of the company.
Source: Interbrand

ACTIVE LONGEST US ROUTE HIGHWAYS

	Highway	Length	Termini
1	Route 20	3,237 miles (5,209 km)	from Newport, OR to Boston, MA
2	Route 6	3,207 miles (5,161 km)	from Bishop, CA to Provincetown, MA
3	Route 30	3,073 miles (4,945 km)	from Astoria, OR to Atlantic City, NJ
4	Route 50	3,011 miles (4,846 km)	from west of Sacramento, CA to Ocean City, MD
5	Route 60	2,670 miles (4,297 km)	from east of Quartzsite, AZ to Virginia Beach, VA
6	Route 2	2,580 miles (4,152 km)	from Everett, WA to St. Ignace, MI
7	Route 12	2,483 miles (3,996 km)	from Aberdeen, WA to Detroit, MI
8	Route 70	2,385 miles (3,838 km)	from Globe, AZ to Atlantic, NC
9	Route 1	2,377 miles (3,825 km)	from Key West, FL to Fort Kent, ME
10	Route 64	2,326 miles (3,743 km)	from Teec Nos Pos, AZ to south of Nags Head, NC

At 2,451 miles (3,944 km), Route 66 would have been #8 on our list, but it was decommissioned in 1985.

HIGHEST-SELLING CAR MODELS EVER

	Model	Total sales (cars sold)	Debut year
1	Toyota Corolla	37.5 million	1966
2	Ford F-Series	35 million	1948
3	Volkswagen Golf	27.5 million	1974
4	Volkswagen Beetle	23.5 million	1933
5	Ford Escort	20 million	1968*
6	Honda Civic	18.5 million	1972
7	Honda Accord	17.5 million	1976
8	Ford Model T	16.5 million	1908‡
9	Volkswagen Passat	15.5 million	1973
10	Chevrolet Impala	14 million	1958

*In production until 2000
‡In production until 1927
Source: 24/7 Wall St.

TOP ICONIC CARS IN MOVIES AND TV

1	The DeLorean	The *Back to the Future* series
2	The General Lee	*The Dukes of Hazzard*
3	The Batmobile	*Batman* (various)
4	KITT	*Knight Rider*
5	The Ectomobile	*Ghostbusters*
6	The Striped Tomato	*Starsky and Hutch*
7	Bullitt's Ford Mustang	*Bullitt*
8	The A-Team Van	*The A-Team*
9	The Bluesmobile	*The Blues Brothers*
10	The Mystery Machine	*Scooby-Doo, Where Are You?*

EARLIEST CARS WITH THREE WHEELS

	Make	Model	Year
1	Benz	Patent Motorwagen	1886*
2	Knight	Tricar	1896
3	Egg & Eggli	Egg	1896
4	Butler	Petrol Cycle	1897
5	Advance	Advance	1902
6	Humber	Tricar	1904
7	Riley Olympia	Tricar	1904
8	Lagonda	Tricar	1904
9	Anglian	Anglian	1905
10	Armadale	Armadale	1906

*Commonly held to be the first real automobile, it was the first car with an internal combustion engine.

PRODUCTION CAR ENGINES WITH THE MOST CYLINDERS

	Manufacturer	Configuration/Cylinders*
1	British Racing Motors	H16
2	British Racing Motors	V16
3	Bugatti Veyron	W16
4	Cadillac	V16
5	Cizeta-Moroder	V16
6	Marmon	V16
7	British Racing Motors	V12
8	Lamborghini	V12
9	Mercedes-Benz	V12
10	Bentley, Ferrari, Life Racing Engines, Napier, Volkswagen	W12

*Ranked by cylinder, alphabetical shape, then maker configuration

FASTEST ACTIVE ROLLER COASTERS

	Name/Park/Location	Speed
1	Formula Rossa/Ferrari World/ Abu Dhabi, UAE	149 mph (240 kph)
2	Kingda Ka/Six Flags Great Adventure/ Jackson Township, NJ	128 mph (206 kph)
3	Top Thrill Dragster/Cedar Point/ Sandusky, OH	120 mph (190 kph)
4	Dodonpa/Fuji-Q Highland/Fujiyoshida, Yamanashi, Japan	107 mph (172 kph)
5=	Superman: Escape from Krypton/ CA Six Flags Magic Mountain/Valencia,	100 mph (160 kph)
5=	Tower of Terror II/Dreamworld/ Coomera, Queensland, Australia	100 mph (160 kph)
7	Steel Dragon 2000/Nagashima Spa Land/Nagashima, Mie, Japan	95 mph (153 kph)
8	Millennium Force/Cedar Point Sandusky, OH	93 mph (150 kph)
9	Leviathan/Canada's Wonderland/ Vaughan, Ontario, Canada	92 mph (148 kph)
10	Intimidator 305/Kings Dominion/ Doswell, VA	90 mph (140 kph)

TALLEST ACTIVE ROLLER COASTERS

	Name/Park/Location	Height
1	Kingda Ka/Six Flags Great Adventure/ Jackson, NJ	456 ft (139 m)
2	Top Thrill Dragster/Cedar Point/ Sandusky, OH	420 ft (130 m)
3	Superman: Escape from Krypton/ Six Flags Magic Mountain/Valencia, CA	415 ft (126 m)
4	Tower of Terror II/Dreamworld/Coomera, Queensland, Australia	377 ft (115 m)
5	Steel Dragon 2000/Nagashima Spa Land/ Nagashima, Mie, Japan	318 ft (97 m)
6	Millennium Force/Cedar Point/ Sandusky, OH	310 ft (94 m)
7	Leviathan/Canada's Wonderland/ Vaughan, Ontario, Canada	306 ft (93 m)
8	Intimidator 305/Kings Dominion/Doswell, VA	305 ft (93 m)
9	Fujiyama/Fuji-Q Highland/ Fujiyoshida, Yamanashi, Japan	259 ft (79 m)
10=	Shambhala: Expedición al Himalaya/ PortAventura/Salou, Catalonia, Spain	249 ft (76 m)
10=	Eejanaika/Fuji-Q Highland/ Fujiyoshida, Yamanashi, Japan	249 ft (76 m)

LONGEST SUBWAY SYSTEMS IN THE WORLD

	Subway system	Length
1	Shanghai	262.9 miles (423.1 km)
2	London	249.8 miles (402 km)
3	New York	228.7 miles (368 km)
4	Beijing	209.4 miles (337 km)
5	Seoul	196.6 miles (316.4 km)
6	Moscow	190.3 miles (306.2 km)
7	Tokyo	189.2 miles (304.5 km)
8	Madrid	177.9 miles (286.3 km)
9	Guangzhou	144.1 miles (231.9 km)
10	Paris	133.6 miles (215 km)

Source: The World Metro Database

FIRST COUNTRIES WITH RAILWAYS

	Country	First railway
1	UK	Sept. 27, 1825
2	France	Nov. 7, 1829
3	USA	May 24, 1830
4	Ireland	Dec. 17, 1834
5	Belgium	May 5, 1835
6	Germany	Dec. 7, 1835
7	Canada	July 21, 1836
8	Russia	Oct. 30, 1837
9	Austria	Jan. 6, 1838
10	Netherlands	Sept. 24, 1839

Although there were earlier horse-drawn railroads, the Stockton & Darlington Railway in the UK inaugurated the world's first steam service. In their early years some of those listed here offered only limited services over short distances, but their opening dates mark the generally accepted beginning of each country's steam railroad system. By 1850, railroads had also begun operating in several other countries, including Italy (1839), Hungary (1846), Denmark (1847), and Spain (1848).

MOST BAD-ASS NAMES FOR US MILITARY AIRCRAFT

	Name	Manufacturer
1	Super Marauder	Martin
2	Chain Lightning	Lockheed
3	Airacuda	Bell
4	Dragon Eye	Aerovironment
5	Skyraider	Douglass
6	Savage	North American
7	Vengeance	Vultee
8	Thunderchief	Republic
9	Fire Scout	Northrop Grumman
10	Goblin	McDonnell

BUSIEST US AIRPORTS

	Airport	Total passenger boardings
1	Hartsfield Jackson Atlanta International Airport	44,414,121
2	O'Hare International Airport	31,892,301
3	Los Angeles International Airport	30,528,737
4	Dallas/Fort Worth International Airport	27,518,358
5	Denver International Airport	25,667,499
6	John F. Kennedy International Airport	23,664,830
7	San Francisco International Airport	20,038,679
8	McCarran International Airport	19,854,759
9	Phoenix Sky Harbor International Airport	19,750,306
10	George Bush Intercontinental Airport	19,306,660

WORST PEACETIME MARINE DISASTERS

	Ship	Number lost	Location	Date
1	MV *Doña Paz*	over 4,000*	Tablas Strait, Philippines	Dec. 20, 1987

The ferry *Doña Paz* was struck by oil tanker MT *Vector*. The official death toll was 1,749, but the *Doña Paz* was overcrowded, with some sources claiming a total of 4,341 lives were lost.

2	SS *Kiangya*	2,750–3,920‡	Off Shanghai, China	Dec. 4, 1948

The overloaded passenger steamship *Kiangya*, carrying Chinese refugees, is believed to have struck a Japanese mine. An estimated 700–1,000 survivors were rescued by other vessels.

3	MV *Le Joola**	over 1,800	Off The Gambia	Sept. 26, 2002

The overcrowded Senegalese ferry capsized in a storm.

4	*Tek Sing*	1,600	Gaspar Strait, Indonesia	Feb. 6, 1822

The large Chinese junk laden with migrant Chinese workers ran aground and sank.

5	SS *Sultana*	1,547	Mississippi River, USA	Apr. 27, 1865

A boiler on the Mississippi steamboat paddlewheeler *Sultana* exploded and the vessel sank. As it occurred soon after the assassination of President Abraham Lincoln, it received little press coverage.

6	RMS *Titanic*	1,517	North Atlantic	Apr. 15, 1912

The most famous marine disaster of all, the *Titanic*, the world's largest liner, sank on her maiden voyage after striking an iceberg.

| 7 | *Toya Maru* | 1,153 | Tsugaru Strait, Japan | Sept. 26, 1954 |

The Japanese ferry between Hokkaido and Honshu sank in a typhoon, with an estimated 150 rescued.

| 8 | SS *General Slocum* | 1,021 | New York, USA | June 15, 1904 |

The excursion steamship caught fire in the East River, New York, with many victims burned or drowned.

| 9 | MS *al-Salam Boccaccio 98* | 1,018• | Red Sea | Feb. 3, 2006 |

The Egyptian car ferry sank following a fire on board.

| 10 | RMS *Empress of Ireland* | 1,012 | Saint Lawrence River Canada | May 29, 1914 |

The Royal Mail ship was struck by Norwegian collier SS *Storstad*, resulting in Canada's worst-ever marine disaster.

*Death tolls vary owing to unmanifested passengers.

‡Stowaways on board make it difficult to pinpoint the exact number of casualties.

•This number is disputed by a few different sources, but 1,018 appears to the figure upon which most agree.

In 1917 the SS *Mont-Blanc* (2,000 dead) accidentally collided with a Norwegian vessel in Halifax, but the deadly explosion was caused by its full cargo of wartime explosives. Similarly, 1,400–2,000 people died in 1707 when four British ships struck dangerous reefs west of the Isles of Scilly, but they were returning from an attack on a French port.

HIGHEST-GROSSING FAST FOOD CHAINS IN THE USA

	Chain	Units*	Sales
1	McDonald's	14,027	$32,395,000
2	Subway‡	23,850	$10,600,000
3	Burger King‡	7,253	$8,600,000
4	Wendy's‡	6,576	$8,340,000
5	Starbucks‡	11,131	$7,560,000
6	Taco Bell	5,634	$6,900,000
7	Dunkin' Donuts‡	6,772	$6,000,000
8	Pizza Hut	7,542	$5,400,000
9	KFC	5,055	$4,700,000
10	Sonic	3,572	$3,619,900

*In 2010
‡Owned and franchised
Source: *QSR* magazine

US FAST FOOD CHAINS WITH THE MOST RESTAURANTS

	Fast food chain	Number of units*
1	Subway	24,722
2	McDonald's	14,098
3	Pizza Hut	7,600
4	Burger King	7,231
5	Dunkin' Donuts	7,015
6	Wendy's	6,594
7	Dairy Queen	6,187
8	Taco Bell	5,670
9	Domino's Pizza	4,907
10	KFC	4,780

*In 2011 (This list covers fast food restaurants, but if it were total restaurants, Starbucks would have been #3 with 10,821.)
Source: *QSR* magazine

TOP 10
BEST-SELLING US BURGER CHAINS

	Company	US sales	Units
1	McDonald's	$32,395,000,000	14,027
2	Burger King*	$8,600,000,000	7,253
3	Wendy's*	$8,340,000,000	6,576
4	Sonic	$3,619,900,000	3,572
5	Jack in the Box	$2,934,800,000	2,206
6	Dairy Queen*	$2,660,000,000	4,514
7	Hardee's*	$1,695,000,000	1,692
8	Carl's Jr.*	$1,310,000,000	1,097
9	Whataburger	$1,225,700,000	717
10	Steak N Shake*	$786,600,000	487

*Includes figures estimated by Technomic, Inc.
Source: *QSR* magazine

TOP BEEF-PRODUCING COUNTRIES

	Country	Market share*
1	USA	25%
2	Brazil	20%
3	European Union	17%
4	China	12%
5=	Argentina	6%
5=	India	6%
7=	Australia	4%
7=	Mexico	4%
9=	Russia	3%
9=	Pakistan	3%

*As of 2010

ANIMALS MOST SLAUGHTERED FOR MEAT IN THE USA

	Meat	Animals slaughtered per annum*
1	Broilers (chicken)	9,323,712,000
2	Turkeys	272,708,000
3	Barrows and gilts	228,705,600
4	Other chickens	167,043,000
5	Steers	36,642,500
6	Heifers	20,479,400
7	Beef cows	6,998,700
8	Dairy cows	6,593,800
9	Sows	6,480,100
10	Lambs and yearlings	4,196,400

*Pound-for-pound, the numbers are much closer, but the animals are not weighed except at the carvery level.
Source: US Department Agriculture

FATTEST US STATES

	State	Proportion of population who are obese
1	Mississippi	34.4%
2	Alabama	32.3%
3	West Virginia	32.2%
4	Tennessee	31.9%
5	Louisiana	31.6%
6	Kentucky	31.5%
7	Oklahoma	31.4%
8	South Carolina	30.9%
9	Arkansas	30.6%
10	Michigan	30.5%

Source: Business Insider

SKINNIEST US STATES

	State	Obesity rate*
1	Colorado	20.7%
2	Hawaii	21.8%
3	Massachusetts	22.7%
4=	New Jersey	23.7%
4=	District of Columbia (Washington D.C.)	23.7%
6	California	23.8%
7	Utah	24.4%
8=	New York	24.5%
8=	Nevada	24.5%
8=	Connecticut	24.5%

*As of 2011
Source: Trust for America's Health, and US Centers for Disease Control and Prevention

COUNTRIES THAT EAT THE MOST FISH

	Country	Consumption per year (in metric tons)
1	China (excl. Taiwan)	13,600,000
2	Japan	9,000,000
3	USA	4,700,000
4	Indonesia	3,600,000
5	India	3,100,000
6	South Korea	2,700,000
7	Thailand	2,400,000
8=	Russia	2,100,000
8=	Philippines	2,100,000
10	Nigeria	1,800,000

Source: *National Geographic*, and *ScienceDaily*

TOP HONEY-PRODUCING COUNTRIES

	Country	Output in metric tons
1	China	398,000
2	Turkey	81,115
3	USA	79,788
4	Ukraine	70,900
5	Argentina	59,000
6	Mexico	55,684
7	Ethiopia	53,675
8	Russia	51,535
9	Iran	47,000
10	India	39,500

Source: Food and Agriculture Organization of the United Nations

HOTTEST CHILIS

	Chili*	Scoville units
1	Naga Jolokia	855,000-1,041,427
2	Red Savina	350,000-577,000
3	Datil, Habanero, Scotch Bonnet	100,000-350,000
4	African Birdseye, Jamaican Hot, Rocoto	100,000-200,000
5	Chiltepin, Malaqueta, Pequin, Santaka, Thai	50,000-100,000
6	Ají, Cayenne, Tabasco	30,000-50,000
7	de Arbol	15,000-30,000
8	Serrano, Yellow Wax	5,000-15,000
9	Chipotle, Jalapeño, Mirasol	2,500-5,000
10	Cascabel, Rocotillo, Sandia, Sriracha	1,500-2,500

*Typical examples – there are others in most categories

Hot peppers contain substances called capsaicinoids, which determine how "hot" they are. In 1912 American pharmacist Wilbur Lincoln Scoville (1865–1942) pioneered a test, based on which chilis are ranked by Scoville units. According to this scale, one part of capsaicin, the principal capsaicinoid, per million equals 15,000 Scoville units. Pure capsaicin registers 15,000,000–17,000,000 on the Scoville scale – one drop diluted with 100,000 drops of water will still blister the tongue – while at the other end of the scale bell peppers and pimento register zero.

US RESTAURANTS WITH 3 MICHELIN STARS

	Restaurant	Chef	City	Year Opened
1	French Laundry	Thomas Keller	Yountville, CA	1978
2	The Restaurant at Meadowood	Christopher Kostow	St. Helena, CA	1979
3	Eleven Madison Park	Daniel Humm	New York, NY	1989
4	Daniel	Daniel Boulud	New York, NY	1993
5	Jean Georges	Mark LaPico	New York, NY	1997
6	Masa	Masa Takayama	New York, NY	2004
7	Per Se	Eli Kaimeh	New York, NY	2004
8	Alinea	Grant Achatz	Chicago, IL	2005
9	Joel Robuchon	Joel Robuchon	Las Vegas, NV	2006
10	Chef's Table at Brooklyn Fare	César Ramírez	New York, NY	2009

Of the 11 restaurants in the United States that have 3 Michelin Stars, Le Bernardin is the oldest, having opened in 1972. However, it did not move from Paris to New York until 1986, and it could be argued that it belongs on this list. The most recent starbearer, Chef's Table at Brooklyn Fare, is New York's only outer-borough restaurant to ever receive the honor.

BEER-SWILLINGEST COUNTRIES

	Country	Gallons consumed annually per capita
1	Czech Republic	38.04
2	Ireland	29.43
3	Germany	27.9
4	Austria	26.58
5	Estonia	26.34
6	Slovenia	25.28
7	Poland	24.75
8	Lithuania	24.36
9	Romania	21.08
10	Bulgaria	20.34

Source: Euromonitor International

BIGGEST BREWING COMPANIES BY SALES

	Beer	Sales (of all beverages made)
1	Anheuser-Busch InBev	$36,297,000,000
2	SABMiller	$28,311,000,000*
3	Heineken	$21,378,600,000
4	Diageo	$20,470,800,000‡•
5	Suntory	$19,629,800,000*•
6	Kirin	$17,236,000,000*•
7	Asahi Group	$16,289,300,000*
8	Carlsberg	$10,683,900,000
9	Grupo Modelo	$6,862,200,000
10	Sapporo	$4,184,800,000*•

*Also makes soft drinks
‡Also makes wine
•Also makes spirits
Source: *Beverage World*
Pernod Ricard would occupy the ninth spot, and Southern Wine & Spirits the tenth, if the criterion were *any* kind of alcohol, but these companies do not brew beer.

THE 10
TOP CRAFT BEERS

1   Goose Island IPA

2   Founder's Breakfast Stout

3   Dogfish Head 90 Minute IPA

4   Victory Prima Pils

5   Live Oak Hefeweizen

6   Avery Mephistopheles' Stout

7   Sierra Nevada Pale Ale

8   Young's Double Chocolate Stout

9   Brooklyn Lager

10   Blue Point Toasted Lager

THE 10

MOST UNUSUAL INGREDIENTS FOUND IN SPECIALTY BEERS

1 **Space Barley**
Sapporo's Space Barley is both the name of their beer, and its main ingredient. That's right - they brewed their beer with barley grown in the vast beyond! As you might expect, this isn't the cheapest beer in Sapporo's portfolio.

2 **Gold**
Some intrepid brewers, such as the folks that made Gordon Finest 24, have started brewing their beer with 24-karat gold. Why? Well... no, seriously... why?

3 **One Thing From Every Continent**
The brewers at Dogfish Head have always thought outside the box. That's why it's no surprise when they unleashed Pangaea on the world. It's brewed with at least one ingredient from every continent.
Yep - even Antarctica.

4 **Key Lime Pie**
In what might be the ultimate dessert beer, Short's Brewing has cooked up a beer with the ingredients for key lime pie, including milk sugar, limes, and graham crackers.

5 **Pizza**
That's right. Pizza. Tom Seefurth's Mamma Mia! Pizza Beer is brewed with one goal in mind - to taste like a pizza. And what better way to do that than to brew with tomatoes, garlic, and pizza spices? As you might expect, it enjoys something of a mixed reputation.

6 **Bulletproof Wood**
While it isn't quite an ingredient, Dogfish Head's Palo Santo Marron is brewed in gigantic vessels made of bulletproof wood. What we're not sure of is: if the wood is bulletproof, then how did they cut it down in the first place?

7 Lemonade
Recently shandy beers—which are part lemonade, part beer—have
been getting more and more popular, especially the iterations put out by
Leinenkugel's and Shock Top. It should be noted that the authors of this
book are at violent odds over this trend.

8 Boysenberries
Speaking of things that shouldn't be within 100 miles of your beer, some
brewers have started experimenting with boysenberries. While most
have tried infusing the flavor in a wheat-based brew, some have gone so
far as to mix it with a pitch black stout.

9 Grape Juice
Going for the hat trick, Dogfish Head once again makes an appearance
on our "Unusual Ingredients" list. Their popular Red and White blends a
wheat beer with pinot noir juice, which is then aged in a wine barrel.

10 Watermelon
Of all the fruits you could use to brew a beer, you wouldn't think
watermelon would be a likely candidate. But recently, breweries such
as the Thomas Hooker Brewing Company and the 21st Amendment
Brewery have enjoyed very popular offerings with watermelon.

BEER WITH HIGHEST ALCOHOL BY VOLUME

	Brewer/beer	Alcohol by volume
1	Brewmeister Armageddon	65%
2	't Koelschip Start the Future	60%
3	Schorschbock 57% Finis Coronat Opus	57%
4	BrewDog End of History	55%
5	BrewDog Sink the Bismarck	41%
6	Struise Black Damnation VI – Messy	39%
7	BrewDog Tactical Nuclear Penguin	32%
8	Mikkeller Heavy Black	31.1%
9=	Hair of the Dog Dave	28%
9=	Hakusekikan Eisbock	28%

Source: iCohol

MOST BITTER BEERS

	Beer	IBUs*
1	Flying Monkeys Alpha Fornication	2,500
2	Mikkeller X Hop Juice 2007 IBU	2,007
3	Hart & Thistle Hop Mess Monster v2.0	1,066
4=	Mikkeller 1000 IBU	1,000
4=	Mikkeller 1000 IBU Barrel Aged	1,000
6	Arbor/Steel City DCLXVI	666
7	To Øl/Mikkeller Overall IIPA	408
8	Struise Black Damnation VI—Messy	340
9	Raasted Festival IPA	335
10	Pitstop The Hop	323

*These beers are measured in IBUs, or International Bittering Units. As a basis for
comparison, Bud Light is around 5-15 IBUs. A pale ale like Sierra Nevada is 38 IBUs.
Source: Beer Tutor

MOST EXPENSIVE BEERS

Beer	Size of bottle	Price
1 Nail Brewing's Antarctic Nail Ale	(500ml)	$800-$1,815

This beer was brewed using ice taken from an Antarctic iceberg.

| 2 BrewDog's The End of History | (330 ml) | $765 |

Only 12 bottles have ever been brewed. And each bottle is stuffed inside a dead animal.

| 3 Carlsberg's Jacobsen Vintage | (375 ml) | $400 |

Each bottle boasts an expiration date of 2059.

| 4 Schorschbräu's Schorschbock 57 | (330 ml) | $27 |

The "57" in the name refers to its 57.5% ABV. Only 36 bottles were made.

| 5 Samuel Adams's Utopias | (700 ml) | $150 |

The alcohol content of this beer (27% ABV) makes it banned in 13 US states.

| 6 Crown Ambassador Reserve | (750 ml) | $90 |

Aged in oak barrels for a year, this Australian beer comes in a champagne bottle.

7   BrewDog's Sink the Bismarck   12 fl oz (375 ml) $80

This beer has an ABV of 41%.

8   Tutankhamun Ale   (500 ml) $75

Recipe derived from beer residue found in ancient Egyptian brewing vessels.

9   BrewDog Tactical   12 fl oz (330 ml) $35–$250
Nuclear Penguin

After being aged in whisky casks for 16 months, this Scottish beer was then exposed to extreme cold to produce its 32% ABV.

10   Pabst Blue Ribbon 1844   (720 ml) $44

Brewed exclusively in China, where it has a much more favorable reputation than in the USA.

Source: Mental Floss

MOST EXPENSIVE WINES

	Wine	Price*
1	Château Cheval Blanc 1947	$304,375
2	Heidsieck 1907	$275,000
3	Château Lafite 1869	$233,972
4	Château Lafite 1787‡	$160,000
5	Romanée-Conti 1945	$123,900
6	Château d'Yquem 1811	$117,000
7	Château Mouton Rothschild 1945	$114,614
8	Château d'Yquem 1784	$56,588
9	Massandra Sherry 1775	$43,500
10	Romanée-Conti, DRC 1990	$28,112

*Sold at auction

‡The reason this wine fetched such an enormous price was that it was part of Thomas Jefferson's private collection. Except it wasn't at all—it was a fake!

TOP 10

MOST EXPENSIVE BOTTLES OF TEQUILA

	Tequila	Price
1	Ultra Premium Tequila Ley .925 Pasión Azteca*	$225,000
2	Barrique de Ponciano Porfidio	$2,000
3	1800 Coleccion	$1,800
4	AsomBroso Reserva Del Porto	$1,100
5	Tres-Quatro-Cinco	$500
6	Rey Sol Anejo	$400
7=	Partida Elegante	$350
7=	Casa Herradua Seleccion Suprema	$350
7=	Don Julio Real	$350
10	Gran Patrón Platinum	$250

*While the tequila inside a bottle of Ultra Premium Tequila Ley .925 Pasión Azteca is distilled from 100% agave and aged for six years, this is not what makes it so expensive. This limited edition of 33 bottles was designed by a Mexican artist and set inside a platinum and white gold bottle. When it was sold at auction in 2006, it set the Guinness World Record for the most expensive bottle of tequila ever sold.
Source: Worldmostexpensive.com

TOP 10

MOST EXPENSIVE SCOTCHES

	Scotch	Price
1	Macallan 64 year old in Lalique	$460,000
2	The Dalmore 64 Trinitas	$160,100
3	The Macallan 1926 Fine and Rare	$75,000
4	The Dalmore 62 Single Hiland Malt Scotch	$58,000
5	Glenfiddich 1937	$20,000
6	The Macallan 55 years old, Lalique Crystal Decanter	$12,500
7	Dalmore 50 years old, Decanter	$11,000
8	Glenfarclas 1955, 50 years old	$10,878
9	The Macallan 1939, 40 years old	$10,125
10	Chivas Regal Royal Salute, 50 years old	$10,000

Source: Worldmostexpensive.com

MOST EXPENSIVE VODKAS

	Vodka	Price*
1	Billionaire Vodka	$3,700,000
2	Russo-Baltique Vodka (New)	$1,350,000
3	Diva Vodka	$1,000,000
4	Russo-Baltique Vodka (Old)	$740,000
5	Belver Bears Vodka	$7,240
6	Oval Vodka	$6,920
7	Iordanov Vodka	$4,353
8	Swarovski-studded Alize Limited Edition	$2,000
9	Absolute Crystal	$1,000
10	Magnum Grey Goose Vodka	$815

*Unlike aged liquors such as scotch, many of the vodkas on this list are priced not because of quality, but because they have intricately designed bottles, which include details like Swarovski crystals or diamonds.
Source: Best Vodka

UNFAMILIAR BEER MEASUREMENTS

1   Snorkel: 2 fluid ounces (57 ml)

Comprising a mere sip, this quick rinse of beer amounts to no more fluid than ends up in one's actual snorkel during an underwater sightseeing trip.

2   Nip: 6.7 fluid ounces (190 ml)

This was a standard size for a bottle of barley wine (which is not a wine but an old-fashioned, dark red, full-bodied beer)—potent enough stuff that this was all one needed. The amount is equal to one-third of a British pint beer mug.

3   Flagon: 40 fluid ounces (1.13 L)

Although in general usage a flagon can be most any size, material, or shape, this is a New Zealand term for a glass container that can be refilled at the local serving establishment. Its existence may stem from a law allowing winemakers to sell their product for consumption later, but only in bulk. It may also be a way to beat the early closing time by law for a period by ordering a flagon or two of beer to take home.

4   Pin: 5.4 gallons (20.5 L)

Essentially a smaller cask, also known as a polypin, this has traditionally been one-eighth the size of a British beer barrel.

5   Anker: 10 gallons (37.85 L)

The anker is an obscure measure of volume of Dutch origin. It equals the amount of beer contained in a small cask holding about 45 bottles.

6   Firkin: 10.8 gallons (41 L)

The beer firkin is only one-eighth the size of a wine firkin! The name means "a fourth" from the Middle Dutch, because a firkin is one-quarter the size of a British beer barrel. This is the prevalent size container for cask ale in Britain.

7 Kilderkin: 21.6 gallons (82 L)

Another Middle Dutch word, the kilderkin equals two firkins. The Dutch have the most fun words to say.

8 Barrel: 31 gallons (117 L)

Finally, something recognizable! If you had a whole barrel of beer, you would have three ways to die, depending on how fast you wanted to do yourself in. You could drown in there and have a nice swim before you do, you could be crushed to death under all that weight of beer, or you could drink yourself to death, which would take anywhere from a couple of days to years. Anyway, that's why there aren't as many working coopers as there used to be: all the customers are done for. Incidentally, a British beer barrel is much bigger than a US beer barrel; British barrels hold 43 gallons (36 imperial gallons, or 164 liters) of beer.

9 Hogshead: 65 gallons (245.5 L)

A hogshead has traditionally equaled one and a half British beer barrels. The name is a source of curiosity to many, but is most likely a corruption of Germanic words meaning "oxhead." That gets us no closer to why anything this big would be named after only the ox's head. Fully packed, a cask this size could easily weigh half a ton, much like certain breeds of cows. You might as well just call it a "Holstein" and represent the entire creature. Today a hogshead of beer is 65 gallons (245.5 liters), while a hogshead of wine is 63 gallons (238.5 liters).

10 Tun: 259 gallons (982 L)

All you need to know is that, yes, the volumetric tun is related to the weight ton (one tun weighs about one ton), and that everything else you could possibly learn about the shifting series of weights and measurements will put you to sleep. Half a tun is a "butt," which is even funnier when you've drank a flagon. One butt equals two hogsheads.

ODDEST COFFEE FLAVORS

	Flavor	Creator
1	Marijuana	Adventurous stoners of the internet
2	Bacon, Egg and Cheese	Nick Kinling
3	Root Beer	Timothy's
4	Carrot Cake	Nature's Coffees
5	Maple Bacon	CoffeeAM
6	Apricot Cream	CoffeeAM
7	Chocolate Raspberry	Sir Wilfred's
8	Egg Nog Rum	CoffeeAM
9	Pumpkin	Green Mountain Coffee
10	Pineapple	Hawaiian Paradise

MOST POPULAR IPAS

	IPA*	Brewery	Average score (out of 5)‡
1	Pliny the Younger	Russian River Brewing Company	4.67
2	Heady Topper	The Alchemist	4.62
3	Pliny the Elder	Russian River Brewing Company	4.59
4	Citra DIPA	Kern River Brewing Company	4.54
5	Bell's Hopslam Ale	Bell's Brewery, Inc.	4.47
6	Double Sunshine IPA	Lawson's Finest Liquids	4.46
7	Double Galaxy	Hill Farmstead Brewery	4.44
8	Ephraim	Hill Farmstead Brewery	4.43
9=	Abrasive Ale	Surly Brewing Company	4.42
9=	Abner	Hill Farmstead Brewery	4.42

*Stands for India Pale Ale; includes both IPAs and Imperial IPAs but does not include pale ales.
‡Based on worldwide user reviews analyzed by BeerAdvocate
Source: BeerAdvocate

LARGEST GREEN-COFFEE PRODUCERS

	Country	Metric tons produced*
1	Brazil	2,874,310
2	Vietnam	1,105,700
3	Indonesia	801,000
4	Colombia	514,128
5	India	289,600
6	Ethiopia	270,000
7	Peru	264,605
8	Guatemala	257,000
9	Mexico	253,800
10	Honduras	229,368

*As of 2010
Source: Food and Agriculture Organization of the United Nations (Faostat)

BEST-SELLING SODA BRANDS

	Brand	Market share*
1	Coke	17%
2	Diet Coke	9.6%
3	Pepsi	9.2%
4	Mountain Dew	6.7%
5	Dr. Pepper	6.4%
6	Sprite	5.7%
7	Diet Pepsi	4.9%
8	Diet Mountain Dew	2.0%
9	Fanta	1.9%
10	Diet Dr. Pepper	1.8%

*In 2011
Source: *Beverage-Digest*

MOST EXPENSIVE CIGARS IN THE WORLD

	Cigar	Price per cigar
1	Gurkha Black Dragon	$1,150
2	Cohiba Behike	$470
3	Arturo Fuente Opus X "A"	$79
4	Fuente Don Arturo AnniverXario	$78
5	King of Denmark	$75
6	Arturo Fuente Opus X BBMF	$55
7	Louixs	$50
8	Stradivarius	$34.70
9	Cohiba Esplendido	$34
10	Padrón Serie 1926 80 Years	$30

Source: Worldmostexpensive.com

NEWEST COUNTRIES

	Country	Date founded
1	The Republic of South Sudan	July 9, 2011
2=	Curaçao*	Oct. 10, 2010
2=	Sint Maarten*	Oct. 10, 2010
4=	The Republic of Abkhazia‡	Aug. 27, 2008
4=	The Republic of South Ossetia‡	Aug. 27, 2008
6	The Republic of Kosovo•	Feb. 17, 2008
7	The Republic of Serbia	June 5, 2006
8	The Republic of Montenegro	June 3, 2006
9	The Democratic Republic of Timor-Leste (East Timor)	May 20, 2002
10	The Republic of Palau	Oct. 1, 1994

*Constituent country of the Kingdom of the Netherlands
‡Recognized by Russia, disputed by Georgia
•Disputed by Serbia
Establishment of a country can be a dodgy matter, so our criterion is the emergence of new borders or clear sovereignty rather than brand-new government.

THE 10
POOREST NATIONS BY GDP (PER CAPITA)

	Nation	GDP per Capita
1	Democratic Republic of Congo	$300
2	Zimbabwe	$500
3	Liberia	$600
4	Somalia	$600
5	Burundi	$600
6	Eritrea	$700
7	Niger	$800
8	Central African Republic	$800
9	Malawi	$900
10	Madagascar	$900

Gross Domestic Product is calculated in international dollars, at purchasing power per capita
Source: CIA World Factboook

MOST POPULATED COUNTRIES

	Nation	Population	Percentage of world population
1	China	1,347,350,000	19.11
2	India	1,210,193,422	17.16
3	USA	314,750,000*	4.46
4	Indonesia	237,641,326	3.37
5	Brazil	193,946,886	2.75
6	Pakistan	180,201,000	2.57
7	Nigeria	166,629,000	2.36
8	Bangladesh	152,518,015	2.16
9	Russia	143,228,300	2.03
10	Japan	127,520,000	1.81

*As of fall 2012

SMALLEST COUNTRIES/ SOVEREIGNTIES BY POPULATION

	Country	Population
1	Pitcairn Islands	66
2	Cocos Islands	550
3	Vatican City	800
4	Niue	1,000*
5	Tokelau	1,411
6	Christmas Island	2,072
7	Norfolk Island	2,302
8	Svalbard and Jan Mayen	2,495
9	Falkland Islands	2,563
10	Saint Helena, Ascension and Tristan da Cunha	4,000*

*UN estimate

COUNTRIES SPENDING THE MOST ON TOURISM

	Country	Tourism spending per capita in 2011 (US $)
1	Germany	78,100,000,000
2	USA	79,100,000,000
3	China	72,600,000,000
4	UK	50,600,000,000
5	France	41,700,000,000
6	Canada	33,000,000,000
7	Russia	32,500,000,000
8	Italy	28,700,000,000
9	Japan	27,200,000,000
10	Australia	26,900,000,000

Source: World Tourism Organization

THE 10
BIGGEST CARBON DIOXIDE POLLUTERS

	Country	Annual carbon dioxide emissions (in metric tons)*	Proportion of world emissions
1	China (excl. Taiwan, Macau, Hong Kong)	7,031,916,000	23.53%
2	USA	5,461,014,000	18.27%
3	European Union	4,177,817,000	13.98%
4	India	1,742,698,000	5.83%
5	Russia	1,708,653,000	5.72%
6	Japan	1,208,163,000	4.04%
7	Germany	786,660,000	2.63%
8	Canada	544,091,000	1.82%
9	Iran	538,404,000	1.80%
10	UK	522,856,000	1.75%

*Based on fossil fuel burning and cement manufacture. Carbon dioxide from other sources was not counted.
Source: United Nations MDG Indicators

LONGEST-REIGNING MONARCHS

	Monarch	Country	Year ascended to throne	Duration of reign
1	Sobhuza II	Swaziland	1899	82 years, 254 days
2	Bernhard VII	Lippe*	1429	81 years, 234 days
3	Wilhelm IV	Henneberg-Schleusingen*	1480	78 years, 243 days
4	Heinrich XI	Reuss-Obergreiz*	1723	77 years, 103 days
5	Christian August	Palatinate-Sulzbach*	1632	75 years, 253 days
6	Muhoji IV Rao	Phaltan (Indi)	1841	74 years, 315 days
7	Bhagvatsingh Sahib	Gondal state (India)	1869	74 years, 87 days
8	Georg Wilhelm	Schaumburg-Lippe	1787	73 years, 282 days
9	Karl Friedrich	Baden	1738	73 years, 29 days
10	John Louis	Nassau-Saarbrücken*	1472	72 years, 228 days

*Sovereign state within the Holy Roman Empire

LONGEST-REIGNING BRITISH MONARCHS

	Monarch	Length of reign
1	Victoria	63 years, 216 days
2	Elizabeth II*	60 years, 208 days
3	George III	59 years, 96 days
4	James VI of Scotland	57 years, 246 days
5	Henry III of England	56 years, 29 days
6	Edward III of England	50 years, 147 days
7	William I of Scotland	48 years, 360 days
8	Llywelyn of Gwynedd (now part of Wales)‡	c. 45 years
9	Elizabeth I of England	44 years, 127 days
10	David II of Scotland	41 years, 260 days

*As of December 2012, Queen ELizabeth II is currently reigning and her figures are not final at the time of this book's publication.
‡Llywelyn's coronation date is unknown, therefore the exact number of years and days is uncertain.

MOST WIDELY SPOKEN NATIVE LANGUAGES

Language		Native speakers	Percentage of world population
1	Mandarin	935 million	14.10
2	Spanish	387 million	5.85
3	English	365 million	5.52
4	Hindi	295 million	4.46
5	Arabic	280 million	4.23
6	Portuguese	204 million	3.08
7	Bengali	202 million	3.05
8	Russian	160 million	2.42
9	Japanese	127 million	1.92
10	Punjabi	95.5 million	1.44

As of September 1, 2012

MOST POPULAR TOURIST NATIONS

	Country	International tourist arrivals in 2011
1	France	79,500,000
2	USA	62,300,000
3	China	57,600,000
4	Spain	56,700,000
5	Italy	46,100,000
6	Turkey	29,300,000
7	UK	29,200,000
8	Germany	28,400,000
9	Malaysia	24,700,000
10	Mexico	23,400,000

Source: World Tourism Organization

COUNTRIES THAT VISIT THE USA MOST OFTEN

	Country	Visitors in 2011
1	Canada	21,300,000
2	Mexico	13,500,000
3	UK	3,800,000
4	Japan	3,200,000
5	Germany	1,800,000
6=	Brazil	1,500,000
6=	France	1,500,000
8=	South Korea	1,100,000
8=	China	1,100,000
10	Australia	1,000,000

Source: International Trade Administration Manufacturing, and Services Office of Travel and Tourism Industries

MOST POWERFUL NUCLEAR TESTS IN THE USA

	Year	Series*
1	1991–1992	Julin
2	1990–1991	Sculpin
3	1989–1990	Aqueduct
4	1988–1989	Cornerstone
5	1987–1988	Touchstone
6	1986–1987	Musketeer
7	1985–1986	Charioteer
8	1984–1985	Grenadier
9	1983–1984	Fusileer
10	1982–1983	Phalanx

*All tests were conducted at the Nevada Test Site. The Total Yield has not been released on any of these tests.

THE DEADLIEST AIR DISASTERS*

	Flight details/Location	Date	Fatalities
1	Terrorist attacks, New York Pennsylvania, Washington D.C.	Sept. 11, 2001	2,996**
2	Tenerife airport disaster, Tenerife, Spain	1977	583
3	Japan Airlines flight 123 (crash), Japan	1985	520
4	Kazakhstan Airlines KZK 1907/ Saudi Arabian Airlines SVA 763 (mid-air collision), Charkhi Dadri, India	1996	349
5	Turkish Airlines flight 981 (crash), France	1974	346
6	Air India flight 182 (bomb), Atlantic Ocean, Ireland	1985	329
7	Iran Ilyushin Il-76 (crash), Iran	2003	302
8	Saudia flight 163 (fire), Riyadh	1980	301
9	Air Africa Antonov An-32 (crash), Kinshasa	1996	300‡
10	Iran Air flight 655 (shot down), Persian Gulf	1988	290

*This list is compiled from non-combat incidents.
**Of this total (which includes the 19 hijackers), 246 were aboard the planes. Three more fatalities were added as a result of conditions caused by dust exposure.
‡Approximate. The plane overshot the runway and crashed into a crowded market.

LONGEST US WAR INVOLVEMENTS

	War	Years of involvement	Duration
1	War in Afghanistan	Oct. 2001–present	10 years, 11 months*
2	Iraq War	Mar. 2003–Dec. 2011	8 years, 9 months
3	Vietnam War	Aug. 1964–Jan. 1973‡	8 years, 5 months
4	American Revolutionary War	Apr. 1775–Sept. 1783	8 years, 5 months
5	American Civil War	Apr. 1861–April 1865	4 years
6	World War II	Dec. 1941–Aug. 1945	3 years, 8 months
7	Korean War	June 1950–July 1953	3 years, 1 month
8	War of 1812	June 1812–Dec. 1814	2 years, 6 months
9	Mexican-American War	May 1846–Feb. 1848	1 year, 9 months
10	World War I	Apr. 1917–Nov. 1918	1 year, 7 months

*As of September 2012
‡The US military was involved in Vietnam from 1950 to 1975, but the Associated Press defines the war as the Gulf of Tonkin Resolution through the Paris Peace Accords.

TALLEST US PRESIDENTS

	President	Height
1=	Abraham Lincoln	6 ft 4 in (193 cm)
1=	Lyndon B. Johnson	6 ft 4 in (193 cm)
3	Thomas Jefferson	6 ft 2½ in (189 cm)
4=	Franklin D. Roosevelt	6 ft 2 in (188cm)
4=	George H. W. Bush	6 ft 2 in (188cm)
4=	Bill Clinton	6 ft 2 in (188cm)
7	George Washington	6 ft 1½ in (187cm)
8=	Andrew Jackson	6 ft 1 in (185 cm)
8=	Ronald Reagan	6 ft 1 in (185 cm)
8=	Barack Obama	6 ft 1 in (185 cm)

SHORTEST US PRESIDENTS

	President	Height
1	James Madison	5 ft 4 in (163 cm)
2=	Martin Van Buren	5 ft 6 in (168 cm)
2=	Benjamin Harrison	5 ft 6 in (168 cm)
4=	John Adams	5 ft 7 in (170 cm)
4=	William McKinley	5 ft 7 in (170 cm)
6	John Quincy Adams	5 ft 7½ in (171 cm)
7=	William Henry Harrison	5 ft 8 in (173 cm)
7=	James K. Polk	5 ft 8 in (173 cm)
7=	Zachary Taylor	5 ft 8 in (173 cm)
7=	Ulysses S. Grant	5 ft 8 in (173 cm)

LONGEST-SERVING US SENATORS

	Senator	Beginning of service	End of service	Days in office
1	Robert C. Byrd (D-WV)	Jan. 3, 1959	June 28, 2010	18,804
2	Daniel K. Inouye (D-HI)	Jan. 3, 1963	Present*	18,139
3	Strom Thurmond (R-SC)‡	Dec. 14, 1954 and Nov. 7, 1956	Apr. 4, 1956 Jan. 3, 2003	17,335
4	Edward M. Kennedy (D-MA)	Nov. 7, 1962	Aug. 25, 2009	17,093
5	Carl T. Hayden (D-AZ)	Mar. 4, 1927	Jan. 3, 1969	15,281
6	John Stennis (D-MS)	Nov. 5, 1947	Jan. 2, 1989	15,034
7	Ted Stevens (R-AK)	Dec. 24, 1968	Jan. 2, 2009	14,619
8	Ernest F. Hollings (D-SC)	Nov. 9, 1966	Jan. 2, 2005	13,934
9	Richard B. Russell (D-GA)	Jan. 12, 1933	Jan. 21, 1971	13,888
10	Russell Long (D-LA)	Dec. 31, 1948	Jan. 2, 1987	13,881

*Still in office as of September 1, 2012
‡Defeated and returned
Source: US Senate

LONGEST-SERVING US REPRESENTATIVES

	Name	Total tenure*
1	John Dingell	56 years, 308 days
2	Jamie L. Whitten	53 years, 60 days
3	Carl Vinson	50 years, 61 days
4	Emanuel Celler	49 years, 305 days
5	Sam Rayburn	48 years, 257 days
6	Sidney R. Yates	48 years, 0 days
7	John Conyers	47 years, 287 days
8	Wright Patman	47 years, 3 days
9	Joseph Gurney Cannon	46 years, 0 days
10	Adolph J. Sabath	45 years, 247 days

*Tenure shown is total years, as of October 17, 2012, including non-consecutive terms. If we were only counting uninterrupted service, Yates and Cannon would be removed from the list, and George H. Mahon and Charles Edward Bennett would be added at joint #9, with each having served exactly 44 years.

THE 10
MOST RECENT*
CONGRESSIONAL MEDAL
OF HONOR RECIPIENTS

	Recipient/Date of issue	Location/date of action
1	Specialist, 4th Class, Leslie H. Sabo, Jr.‡ (May 16, 2012)	Se San, Cambodia, May 10, 1970
2	Sergeant Dakota Meyer (Sept. 15, 2011)	Kunar Province, Afghanistan, Sept. 8, 2009
3	Staff Sergeant Leroy Petry (July 12, 2011)	Paktya Province, Afghanistan, May 26, 2008
4=	PFC Anthony T. Kaho'ohanohano‡ (May 2, 2011)	Chupa-ri, Korea , Sept. 1, 1951
4=	PFC Henry Svehla‡ (May 2, 2011)	Pyongony, Korea, June 12, 1952
6	Staff Sergeant Salvatore A. Giunta (Nov. 16, 2010)	Korengal Valley, Afghanistan, Oct. 25, 2007
7	Staff Sergeant Robert J. Miller‡ (Oct. 6, 2010)	Kunar Province, Afghanistan, Jan. 25, 2008
8	Chief Master Sergeant Richard L. Etchberger‡ (Sept. 21, 2010)	Phou Pha Thi, Laos, Mar. 11, 1968
9	Sergeant First Class Jared C. Monti‡ (Sept. 17, 2009)	Nuristan Province, Afghanistan, June 21, 2006
10	PFC Ross A. McGinnis‡ (June 5, 2008)	Adhamiyah, Northeast Baghdad, Iraq, Dec. 4, 2006

*As of September 1, 2012
‡Soldier fell in battle

TOP 10

RICHEST US STATES BY HOUSEHOLD INCOME

	State	Median household income*
1	Maryland	$70,004
2	Alaska	$67,825
3	New Jersey	$67,458
4	Connecticut	$65,753
5	Massachusetts	$62,859
6	New Hampshire	$62,647
7	Virginia	$61,882
8	Hawaii	$61,821
9	Delaware	$58,814
10	California	$57,287

*In other words, half the households in the state have an income above this figure and half below this figure.
If the District of Columbia were included, it would be #5, at $63,124.

POOREST US STATES BY HOUSEHOLD INCOME

	State	Median household income*
1	Mississippi	$36,919
2	West Virginia	$38,482
3	Arkansas	$38,758
4	Kentucky	$41,141
5	Alabama	$41,415
6	Tennessee	$41,693
7	Louisiana	$41,734
8	New Mexico	$41,963
9	South Carolina	$42,367
10	Oklahoma	$43,225

*In other words, half the households in the state have an income above this figure and half below this figure.

US STATES WITH THE YOUNGEST POPULATION

	Stage	Median age in years*
1	Utah	29.2
2	Texas	33.6
3	Alaska	33.8
4	Idaho	34.6
5	California	35.2
6	Georgia	35.3
7	Louisiana	35.8
8	Arizona	35.9
9	Kansas	36.0
10	Mississippi	36.0

*In other words, half the population of the stage is above this age, and half below.
If the District of Columbia were included, it would take the #4 spot, with a median
age of 33.8 years.
Source: US Census

US STATES WITH THE OLDEST POPULATION

	State	Median age in years*
1	Maine	42 .7
2	Vermont	41 .5
3	West Virginia	41 .3
4	New Hampshire	41 .1
5	Florida	40 .7
6	Pennsylvania	40 .1
7	Connecticut	40 .0
8	Montana	39 .8
9	Rhode Island	39 .4
10	Massachusetts	39 .1

*Half the population of the stage is above this age, and half below.
Source: US Census

US STATES WITH MOST FOREIGN-BORN RESIDENTS

	State	Percentage of state population
1	California	26.9
2	New York	21.4
3	New Jersey	20.2
4	Nevada	19.2
5	Florida	18.8
6	Hawaii	17.3
7	Texas	16.1
8	Massachusetts	14.3
9	Arizona	14.0
10	Illinois	13.5

Source: US Census

US STATES WITH FEWEST FOREIGN-BORN RESIDENTS

	State	Percentage of state population
1	West Virginia	1.3
2=	Mississippi	2.0
2=	Montana	2.0
4	North Dakota	2.4
5	South Dakota	2.7
6	Kentucky	3.0
7=	Wyoming	3.1
7=	Alabama	3.1
9=	Vermont	3.3
9=	Maine	3.3

Source: US Census

LEAST POPULOUS US STATES

	State	Population
1	Wyoming	563,626
2	Vermont	625,741
3	North Dakota	672,591
4	Alaska	710,231
5	South Dakota	814,180
6	Delaware	897,934
7	Montana	989,415
8	Rhode Island	1,052,567
9	New Hampshire	1,316,470
10	Maine	1,328,361

Source: US Census

MOST POPULOUS US STATES

	State	Population
1	California	37,253,956
2	Texas	25,145,561
3	New York	19,378,102
4	Florida	18,801,310
5	Illinois	12,830,632
6	Pennsylvania	12,702,379
7	Ohio	11,536,504
8	Michigan	9,883,640
9	Georgia	9,687,653
10	North Carolina	9,535,483

Source: US Census

BIGGEST AGRICULTURAL EXPORTER US STATES

	State	2010 agricultural export
1	California	$14,060,800,000
2	Iowa	$9,507,600,000
3	Illinois	$7,785,300,000
4	Texas	$6,933,900,000
5	Nebraska	$6,584,100,000
6	Minnesota	$6,078,000,000
7	Kansas	$4,818,400,000
8	Indiana	$4,501,200,000
9	Missouri	$3,519,500,000
10	Ohio	$3,456,500,000

Source: Food and Agriculture Organization of the United Nations

OLDEST EXTANT CITIES IN THE USA

	Year	City	State
1=	1000	Acoma Pueblo*	New Mexico
1=	1000	Taos Pueblo	New Mexico
3	1100	Oraibi	Arizona
4	1450	Zuni Pueblo	New Mexico
5	1565	Saint Augustine	Florida
6	1585	Roanoke Colony	Virginia
7=	1607	Santa Fe	New Mexico
7=	1607	Jamestown	Virginia
9=	1610	Kecoughtan	Virginia
9=	1610	Hampton	Virginia

*Now known as Sky City

Cahokia, Illinois, is the oldest extant city in America, but was abandoned in the 1300s, and resettled by Europeans in the late 17th century, so its existence has not been continuous.

MOST POPULOUS US CITIES

	City	Population
1	New York City	8,175,133
2	Los Angeles	3,792,621
3	Chicago	2,695,598
4	Houston	2,099,451
5	Philadelphia	1,526,006
6	Phoenix	1,445,632
7	San Antonio	1,327,407
7	San Diego	1,307,402
7	Dallas	1,197,816
10	San Jose	945,962

BIZARRE SMALL-TOWN SLOGANS IN THE USA

	Town	Slogan
1	Gettysburg, South Dakota	"Where the battle wasn't"
2	Peculiar, Missouri	"Where the odds are with you"
3	San Andreas, California	"It's not our fault"
4	Gas, Kansas	"Don't pass Gas, stop and enjoy it"
5	Beaver, Oklahoma	"Cow chip capital"
6	Cherryfield, Maine	"Blueberry capital of the world"
7	Weed, California	"Weed like to welcome you"
8	Claxton, Georgia	"Fruitcake capital of the world"
9	Jefferson, Wisconsin	"The Gemütlichkeit* city"
10	Madisonville, Kentucky	"The best town on Earth"

*Reflecting Wisconsin's German heritage, *Gemütlichkeit* is a German word meaning a quality of coziness and amiability.

QUIRKY SMALL TOWN NAMES IN THE USA

Town

1 Intercourse, Alabama

Originally named for a street intersection (which was then known as an "intercourse") near the general store, the community has been identifying itself by other names these days.

2 Mexican Hat, Utah

Named after a nearby rock formation that is shaped somewhat similarly to a sombrero.

3 Bad Axe, Michigan

The two surveyors who founded this town discovered an old, damaged axe at the site of their camp. They "temporarily" called the site "Bad Axe Camp." Over 150 years ago.

4 Knockemstiff, Ohio

There are many stories about the origin of Knockemstiff's name. Most are about fighting. One is about moonshine.

5 Embarrass, Wisconsin

French Canadian lumberjacks named the village after the French phrase "*Rivière Embarrassée*," because there were a lot of snags and debris stopping logs from floating down the river.

6   Humptulips, Washington

Nobody is quite sure where this name came from. Some think it came
from a Native American term meaning "hard to pole" (referring to
difficulty poling along the river). It may have also meant "chilly region"
or have been the nickname for the Chehalis tribe.

7   Truth or Consequences, New Mexico

Originally named Hot Springs, this town changed its name in order to win
a contest put on by *Truth or Consequences*, a popular NBC radio program.

8   Greasy Corner, Arkansas

Named for a store that was a store, restaurant, and auto mechanic all
in one.

9   Zzyzx, California

Given as a made-up name and as the "last word in the English
language."

10   No Name, Colorado

After I-70 was constructed, a DOT employee went out to improve
signage. Upon noticing that the area didn't have an official title, he simply
put "No Name" on the exit sign. The name stands to this day.

Source: itsallgood.itgo.com

MOST EXPENSIVE PRIVATE BOATS

	Name	Owner	Cost ($)
1	History Supreme	Unknown	4.8 billion
2	Street of Monaco	Unknown	1.1 billion
3	Eclipse	Roman Abromovich	1 billion
4	Dubai	Sheik Mohanned bin Rashid Al Maktoum	350 million
5	Superyacht A	Andrey Melnichenko	323 million
6	Al Said	Said al Said	300 million
7	Dilbar	Unknown	256 million
8	Al Mirqab	Sheikh Hama bin Jassim bin Jaber Al-Thani	250 million
9	Lady Moura	Nasser al-Rashid	210 million
10	Rising Sun	Larry Ellison, David Geffen	200 million

LARGEST LOTTERY JACKPOTS IN THE USA

	Payout (£ million)	Lottery game	Date	State of ticket holder(s)
1	$656	Mega Millions	Mar. 30, 2012	Kansas, Illinois, Maryland
2	$390	Mega Millions	Mar. 6, 2007	Georgia, New Jersey
3	$380	Mega Millions	Jan. 4, 2011	Idaho, Washington
4	$365	Powerball	Feb. 18, 2006	Nebraska
5	$363	The Big Game	May 9, 2000	Illinois, Michigan
6	$340	Powerball	Oct. 19, 2005	Oregon‡
7	$336	Mega Millions	Aug. 28, 2009	California, New York
8	$331	The Big Game	Apr. 16, 2002	Georgia, Illinois, New Jersey
9	$330	Mega Millions	Aug. 31, 2007	New Jersey, Maryland, Texas, Virginia
10	$319	Mega Millions	Mar. 25, 2011	New York

*Won by Holly Lahti of Rathdrum, Idaho; Jim and Carolyn McCullar of Ephrata, Washington
‡Won by the Chaney and West families

TOP OIL-PRODUCING COUNTRIES

	Country	Barrels produced per day
1	Saudi Arabia	11,153,000
2	Russia	10,229,000
3	USA	10,142,000
4	China	4,299,000
5	Iran	4,234,000
6	Canada	3,660,000
7	United Arab Emirates	3,096,000
8	Mexico	2,959,000
9	Brazil	2,687,000
10	Kuwait	2,682,000

As of 2011
Source: US Energy Information Administration (EIA)

THE 10
TOP OIL-PRODUCING US STATES

	State	Barrels produced per month
1	Texas	59,675,000
2	North Dakota	20,896,000
3	California	16,430,000
4	Alaska	12,873,000
5	New Mexico	7,014,000
6	Oklahoma	6,890,000
7	Louisiana	5,917,000
8	Wyoming	5,077,000
9	Colorado	3,684,000
10	Kansas	3,643,000

As of June 2012
Source: US Energy Information Administration (EIA)

TOP SILVER-PRODUCING COUNTRIES

	Country	Silver production in 2011
1	Mexico	152,800,000 oz (4,331,880 kg)
2	Peru	109,800,000 oz (3,112,830 kg)
3	China	103,900,000 oz (2,945,565 kg)
4	Australia	55,200,000 oz (1,564,920 kg)
5	Chile	42,100,000 oz (1,193,535 kg)
6	Poland	40,800,000 oz (1,156,680 kg)
7	Russia	40,000,000 oz (1,134,000 kg)
8	Bolivia	39,000,000 oz (1,105,650 kg)
9	USA	36,000,000 oz (1,020,600 kg)
10	Argentina	22,600,000 oz (640,710 kg)

Source: The Silver Institute

MOST WIDELY GROWN CROPS IN THE USA

	Commodity	Production (value)	Production (metric tons)
1	Maize	$26,714,587,000	316,165,000
2	Soybeans	$23,575,706,000	90,605,500
3	Wheat	$8,593,450,000	60,062,400
4	Cotton lint	$5,633,493,000	3,941,700
5	Tomatoes	$4,752,113,000	12,858,700
6	Almonds	$4,172,080,000	1,413,800
7	Grapes	$3,874,266,000	6,777,730
8	Rice	$3,019,697,000	11,027,000
9	Potatoes	$2,886,295,000	18,337,500
10	Lettuce and chicory	$1,919,412,000	4,105,580

Source: Food and Agriculture Organization of the United Nations

COUNTRIES THAT CATCH THE MOST FISH

	Country	Fish caught (in metric tons)
1	China (except Taiwan)	9,900,000
2	Peru	8,300,000
3	USA	4,900,000
4	Japan	4,400,000
5=	Chile	4,200,000
5=	Indonesia	4,200,000
7	India	3,400,000
8	Russia	3,100,000
9=	Thailand	2,600,000
9=	Norway	2,600,000

Source: *National Geographic*

NEWEST PERIODIC ELEMENTS

	Atomic number	Name	Symbol
1	118	Ununoctium*	Uuo
2	117	Ununseptium*	Uus
3	116	Livermorium	Lv
4	115	Ununpentium*	Uup
5	114	Flerovium	Fl
6	113	Ununtrium*	Uut
7	112	Copernicium	Cn
8	111	Roentgenium	Rg
9	110	Darmstadtium	Ds
10	109	Meitnerium	Mt

*Temporary name

MOST COMMON METALS IN THE HUMAN BODY

	Metal	Percentage of mass:
1	Calcium	1.4
2	Potassium	.25
3	Sodium	.15
4	Magnesium	.05
5	Iron	.006
6	Zinc	.0032
8	Strontium	.00046
7	Rubidium	.00046
9	Lead	.00017
10	Copper	.0001

COLDEST DAYS IN US HISTORY

	Temperature	Place	Date
1	–80°F (–62°C)	Prospect Creek Camp, Alaska	Jan. 23, 1971
2	–70°F (–57°C)	Rogers Pass, Montana	Jan. 20, 1954
3	–69°F (–56°C)	Peter's Sink, Utah	Feb. 1, 1985
4	–66°F (–54°C)	Riverside R.S., Wyoming	Feb. 9, 1933
5	–61°F (–52°C)	Maybell, Colorado	Feb. 1, 1985
6=	–60°F (–51°C)	Island Park Dam, Idaho	Jan. 18, 1943
6=	–60°F (–51°C)	Tower, Minnesota	Feb. 2, 1996
6=	–60°F (–51°C)	Parshall, North Dakota	Feb. 15, 1936
9	–58°F (–50°C)	McIntosh, South Dakota	Feb. 17, 1936
10	–55°F (–48°C)	Couderay, Wisconsin	Feb. 4, 1996

HURRICANES WITH STRIPPERS' NAMES

	Name	Most Recent Year
1	Jasmine	2012
2	Cleo	2009
3	Crystal	2002
4	Ginger	1997
5	Babie	1992
6	Aurora	1983
7	Trixie	1974
8	Emmanuelle	1973
9	Gigi	1972
10	Jackie	1967

WETTEST CITIES IN THE CONTINENTAL USA

	City	Average annual rainfall
1	Mobile, Alabama	67 inches (170 cm)
2	Pensacola, Florida	65 inches (165 cm)
3	New Orleans, Louisiana	64 inches (163 cm)
4	West Palm Beach, Florida	63 inches (160 cm)
5=	Lafayette, Louisiana	62 inches (157 cm)
5=	Baton Rouge, Louisiana	62 inches (157 cm)
5=	Miami, Florida	62 inches (157 cm)
8=	Port Arthur, Texas	61 inches (155 cm)
8=	Tallahassee, Florida	61 inches (155 cm)
10	Lake Charles, Louisiana	58 inches (147 cm)

Source: Live Science

THE 10
MOST EXPENSIVE HURRICANES IN US HISTORY

	Hurricane	Year	Category*	Cost
1	*Katrina* (SE Florida, Louisiana, Missouri)	2005	3	$108,000,000,000
2	*Ike* (Texas, Louisiana)	2008	2	$29,520,000,000
3	*Andrew* (SE Florida, Louisiana)	1992	5	$26,500,000,000
4	*Wilma* (S Florida)	2005	3	$21,007,000,000
5	*Ivan* (Alabama, NW Florida)	2004	3	$18,820,000,000
6	*Charley* (SW Florida)	2004	4	$15,113,000,000
7	*Rita* (SW Louisiana, N Texas)	2005	3	$12,037,000,000
8	*Frances* (Florida)	2004	2	$9,507,000,000
9	*Allison* (N Texas)	2001	TS‡	$9,000,000,000
10	*Jeanne* (Florida)	2004	3	$7,660,000,000

*Category 1 is 74–95 mph (119–153 kph), category 2 is 96–110 mph (154–177 kph), category 3 is 111–130 mph (178–209 kph), category 4 is 131–155 mph (210–249 kph), and category 5 is greater than 155mph (249 kph).
‡Technically, *Allison* was a tropical storm, not a hurricane.
At the time of publication, the total cost of hurricane *Sandy* was still being calculated, but it is estimated to be around the $50 or $60 billion mark. This would put it at #2 of all time.
Source: National Hurricane Center

DEADLIEST HURRICANES IN US HISTORY

	Hurricane	Year	Category*	Deaths
1	Texas (Galveston)	1900	4	8,000
2	Florida (SE/Lake Okeechobee)	1928	4	2,500
3	*Katrina* (SE Louisiana, Missouri)	2005	3	1,200
4	Louisiana (Cheniere Caminanda)	1893	4	1,100-1,400
5	South Carolina/Georgia (Sea Islands)	1893	3	1,000-2,000
6	Georgia/South Carolina	1881	2	700
7	*Audrey* (SW Louisiana/N Texas)	1957	4	416
8	Florida (Keys)	1935	5	408
9	Louisiana (Last Island)	1856	4	400
10	Florida (Miami, Pensacola)/ Missouri/Alabama	1926	4	372

*Category 1 is 74–95 mph(119–153 kph), category 2 is 96–110 mph (154–177 kph), category 3 is 111–130 mph (178–209 kph), category 4 is 131–155 mph (210–249 kph), and category 5 is greater than 155mph (249 kph).
Source: National Hurricane Center

MOST RECENT RETIRED HURRICANE NAMES

	Hurricane	Year retired*
1	*Irene*	2011
2=	*Igor*	2010
2=	*Thomas*	2010
4=	*Gustav*	2008
4=	*Ike*	2008
4=	*Paloma*	2008
7=	*Dean*	2007
7=	*Felix*	2007
7=	*Noel*	2007
10=	*Dennis*	2005
10=	*Katrina*	2005
10=	*Rita*	2005
10=	*Stan*	2005
10=	*Wilma*	2005

*A name is removed from the official list of names for future hurricanes if the World Meteorological Organization decides that a storm has been so deadly or costly that the subsequent use of its name would be inappropriate.
Source: National Hurricane Center

CLOSEST STARS

	Star*	Distance in light years‡
1	Proxima Centauri	4.2421
2=	Alpha Centauri A	4.3650
2=	Alpha Centauri B	4.3650
4	Barnard's Star	5.9630
5	Wolf 359	7.7825
6	Lalande 21185	8.2905
7=	Sirius A	8.5828
7=	Sirius B	8.5828
9=	Luyten 726-8 A	8.7280
9=	Luyten 726-8 B	8.7280

*Does not include the sun
‡A light year is a unit of distance equal to the distance that light travels in one year.

LARGEST CONSTELLATIONS

	Constellation	Area (in square degrees*)
1	Hydra	1,302.844
2	Virgo	1,294.428
3	Ursa Major	1,279.660
4	Cetus	1,231.411
5	Hercules	1,225.148
6	Eridanus	1,137.919
7	Pegasus	1,120.794
8	Draco	1,082.952
9	Centaurus	1,060.422
10	Aquarius	979.854

*A square degree is a unit for measuring parts of a sphere.

SMALLEST STARS IN THE KNOWN UNIVERSE

	Star	Solar radii*
1	Beta Cygni B	.14
2	Sirius B	.21
3	Gliese 229	.31
4	Proxima Centauri	.46
5	G103 Cephei	.49
6	Luyten's Star	.73
7	Alpha Centauri B	.94
8	Sun	1
9	Alpha Centauri A	1.38
10	Sirius	6.41

*A solar radius is a unit of distance, equal to the distance from the center of the sun to the edge, which allows us to compare the size of a star with the size of the sun.
Source: The Universe Data

LARGEST STARS IN THE KNOWN UNIVERSE

	Star	Size in solar radii*
1	NML Cygni	1,650
2	V838 Monocerotis	1,570 ± 400
3	WOH G64	1,540
4	VX Sagittarii	1,520
5	KW Sagittarii	1,460
6=	KY Cygni	1,420
6=	VY Canis Majoris	1,420
8	RW Cephei	1,260
9	PZ Cassiopeiae	1,190
10	VV Cephei A	1,050

*Estimated sizes. A solar radius is a unit of distance, equal to the distance from the center of the sun to the edge, which allows us to compare the size of a star with the size of the sun.

US STATES WITH HIGHEST BIRTH RATES

	State	Birth rate per 1,000
1	Utah	18.907
2	Alaska	16.151
3	Texas	15.355
4	Washington, D.C.	15.231
5	Idaho	14.799
6	South Dakota	14.507
7	Kansas	14.247
8	Oklahoma	14.192
9	Nebraska	14.191
10	Hawaii	13.959

Source: US Centers for Disease Control and Prevention, and US Census

THE 10
US STATES WITH LOWEST BIRTH RATES

	State	Births	Population	Birth rate per 1,000
1	New York	151,528	19,378,102	7.820
2	Maine	12,970	1,328,361	9.764
3	New Hampshire	12,874	1,316,470	9.779
4	Vermont	6,223	625,741	9.945
5	Connecticut	37,708	3,574,097	10.550
6	Rhode Island	11,177	1,052,567	10.619
7	West Virginia	20,470	1,852,994	11.047
8	Massachusetts	72,865	6,547,629	11.128
9	Pennsylvania	143,321	12,702,379	11.283
10	Florida	214,590	18,801,310	11.414

Source: US Centers for Disease Control and Prevention, and US Census

MOST POPULAR BABY NAMES IN THE USA*

	Male name	Female name
1	Jacob	Sophia
2	Mason	Isabella
3	William	Emma
4	Jayden	Olivia
5	Noah	Ava
6	Michael	Emily
7	Ethan	Abigail
8	Alexander	Madison
9	Aiden	Mia
10	Daniel	Chloe

In 2011
*Per the US Social Security Administration: "All data are from a 100% sample of [the Social Security Administration's] records on Social Security card applications as of the end of February 2012."
Source: US Social Security Administration

LARGEST US ANCESTRIES

	Ancestry	Population
1	German	50,707,758
2	Irish	36,915,155
3	English	27,657,961
4	American	18,699,411
5	Italian	18,085,336
6	Polish	10,091,056
7	French	9,411,789
8	Scottish	5,847,063
9	Dutch	5,023,846
10	Norwegian	4,642,526

Source: US Census

US RELIGIOUS BELIEFS

	Religion	Adherents
1	Christians	257,935,642
2	Agnostics	38,695,319
3	Jews	5,241,553
4	Muslims	4,805,776
5	Buddhists	4,047,598
6	New religionists	1,662,922
7	Hindus	1,478,555
8	Atheists	1,328,803
9	Ethnoreligionists	1,109,997
10	Baha'is	525,046

Source: World Christian Database

TOP 10

SMALLEST MULTIPLE-CHURCH RELIGIONS ON RECORD IN THE USA

	Religious body	Year reported	Churches reported	Membership
1	Grace Gospel Fellowship	1992	128	60,000
2	Polish National Catholic Church of America	2008	126	60,000
3	IFCA International, Inc.	1998	659	61,655
4	The Alliance of Baptists	2006	127	65,000
5	Armenian Apostolic Church, Diocese of America	2008	63	65,000
6	National Association of Congregational Christian Churches	2001	432	65,392
7	Cumberland Presbyterian Church	2009	643	65,591
8	Serbian Orthodox Church in the USA. and Canada	2005	68	67,000
9	International Council of Community Churches	2009	137	69,276
10	Free Methodist Church of North America	2009	1,053	75,586

Source: US Census
The US Census does not record religion but did collect the information from those churches that voluntarily gave it for the Statistical Abstract. Doubtless, there are countless smaller churches that did not make themselves known. Take another grain of salt for the broad variance in year of reporting, as many are subject to immigration trends.

LEADING CAUSES OF INJURY IN THE USA

	Product/activity	Estimated annual injuries
1	Beds, mattresses, pillows	531,280
2	Basketball	512,213
3	Bicycles and accessories	494,712
4	Chairs, sofas, sofa beds	453,424
5	Football	418,260
6	Tables	298,949
7	Bathroom structures and fixtures	293,432
8	Baseball, softball	262,529
9	ATVs, mopeds, minibikes, etc.	250,553
10	Exercise, exercise equipment	243,751

Source: Consumer Product Safety Council, National Electronic Injury Surveillance System

MOST ANNOYING CO-WORKERS

1   Machiavelli
    This fellow thinks himself the master of an office teeming with other conniving power-mongers.

2   Lone Wolf
    Driven to succeed...just not with the rest of the team.

3   Clueless Boss
    You can't lead if you're riding backward on your horse.

4   Brown-Noser
    Yes-men are half the reason #3 is so clueless.

5   Gossip
    Knows everyone else's business before they do, even if the truth gets lost along the way.

6   Layabout
    Does maybe one solid hour of work a day.

7   Overly Friendly Boss
    Wants to be your pal at the cost of meeting project goals.

8   The Egomaniac
    These people are the worst anywhere, but especially complimenting themselves on your hard work.

9   The Ergomaniac
    So concerned with efficiency and ease, they never actually save any time, money or comfort.

10 You
    Nobody's perfect. You sit here and judge the nine members of your team.

TOP CULTURAL HOLIDAYS CELEBRATED IN US

	Holiday	Country/Region	Date
1	St Patrick's Day	Ireland	Mar. 17
2	Chinese New Year	China	Late Jan./Early Feb.
3	Kwanzaa	Africa	Dec. 26–Jan.1
4	Cinco de Mayo	Mexico	May 5
5	Puerto Rican Day	Puerto Rico	Second Sunday of June
6	Oktoberfest	Germany/Austria	Late Sept./Mid Oct.
7	Mardi Gras	French colonial	Late Feb./Early March
8	Dominican Day	Dominican Republic	Early/Mid Aug.
9	Victory Day	Russia	May 9
10	Nowruz	Persian & more	Vernal equinox

THE 10
SELF-MADE WEALTHIEST WOMEN

Name	Career

1. Wu Yajun — Founder, Longfor Properties
A journalist turned real estate developer, Yajun's wealth has exploded to $5.7 bn.

2. Sara Blakely — Founder, Spanx
This Florida native designed stockings friendlier to hot-weather shoes.

3. Oprah Winfrey — TV star
The talk how host and media juggernaut overcame brutal childhood experiences to wield unmatched influence.

4. JK Rowling — Author
When the author began the *Harry Potter* series, she was a single mother on welfare living in an Edinburgh flat.

5. Doris Fisher — Founder, The Gap
Fisher presides over a clothing empire that includes Banana Republic and Old Navy.

6. Madonna — Musician
The world-famous vixen once hustled cassette tapes of her demo in front of New York DJs until they agreed to play her music.

7. Coco Chanel — Founder, Chanel
Born of French peasants and reared in a convent, this beauty plied her trade as a seamstress into the highest level of fashion.

8. Josie Natori — Founder/CEO, The Natori Co.
After migrating from the Philippines to Westchester, NY to attend college, she abandoned investment banking to create high-end women's lingerie.

9. Shama Kabani — Founder/CEO, The Marketing Zen Gp
A social media marketer who has seen her worth swell 400% each year.

10. Deanna Jump — Founder, Teachers Pay Teachers
This Georgia teacher developed a way for her profession to share creative, engaging lesson plans. The first year she only made $300.

VERIFIED OLDEST PEOPLE

	Name	Born/Died	Age
1	Jeanne Calment	Feb. 21, 1875/ Aug. 4, 1997	122 years,164 days
2	Sarah Knauss	Sept. 24, 1880/ Dec. 30, 1999	119 years, 97 days
3	Lucy Hannah	July 16,1875/ Mar. 21, 1993	117 years, 248 days
4	Marie-Louise Meilleur	Aug. 29, 1880/ Apr. 16,1998	117 years, 230 days
5	Marìa Capovilla	Sept. 14, 1889/ Aug. 27, 2006	116 years, 347 days
6	Tane Ikai	Jan. 18, 1879/ July 12, 1995	116 years 175 days
7	Elizabeth Bolden	Aug. 15, 1890/ Dec. 11, 2006	116 years, 118 day
8	Besse Cooper	Aug. 26, 1896/ Dec. 4, 2012	116 years, 100 days
9	Maggie Barnes	Mar. 6, 1882/ Jan. 19, 1998	115 years, 319 days
10	Christian Mortensen	Aug. 16, 1882/ Apr. 25, 1998	115 years, 252 days

Two other women, Carrie C. White and Kamato Hongo, would have been #8 and #9 on this list, but there are disputes regarding how old both actually were at the time of their deaths.

OLDEST PEOPLE WHO LIVED IN THREE CENTURIES

	Name	Born/Died	Age
1	María Capovilla	Sept. 14, 1889/ Aug. 27, 2006	116 years, 347 days
2	Elizabeth Bolden	Aug. 15, 1890/ Dec. 11, 2006	116 years, 118 days
3	Besse Cooper	Aug. 26, 1896/ Living	116 years, 79 days*
4	Dina Manfredini	Apr. 4, 1897/ Living*	115 years, 223 days
5	Edna Parker	Apr. 20, 1893/ Nov. 26, 2008	115 years, 220 days
6	Jiroemon Kimura	Apr. 19, 1897/ Living	115 years, 208 days*
7	Gertrude Baines	Apr. 6, 1894/ Sept. 11, 2009	115 years, 158 days
8	Emiliano Mercado del Toro	Aug. 21, 1891/ Jan. 24, 2007	115 years, 156 days
9	Bettie Wilson	Sept. 13, 1890/ Feb. 13, 2006	115 years, 153 days
10	Julie Winnefred Bertrand	Sept. 16, 1891/ Jan. 18, 2007	115 years, 124 days

*As of November 13, 2012

COUNTRIES WITH HIGHEST LIFE EXPECTANCIES

	Country/territory*	Life expectancy in 2012
1	Monaco	89.68
2	Macau	84.43
3	Japan	83.91
4	Singapore	83.75
5	San Marino	83.07
6	Andorra	82.50
7	Guernsey	82.24
8	Hong Kong	82.12
9	Australia	81.90
10	Italy	81.86

*Includes non-sovereign entities
Source: CIA World Factbook (2011 estimates)

COUNTRIES WITH LOWEST LIFE EXPECTANCIES

	Country	Life expectancy in 2012
1	Chad	48.69
2	Guinea-Bissau	49.11
3	South Africa	49.41
4	Swaziland	49.42
5	Afghanistan	49.72
6	Central African Republic	50.48
7	Somalia	50.80
8	Zimbabwe	51.82
9	Lesotho	51.86
10	Mozambique	52.02

Source: CIA World Factbook (2011 estimates)

US STATES WITH HIGHEST MALE LIFE EXPECTANCY

	State	Male life expectancy (in years)
1	Utah	78.8
2	Minnesota	78.5
3=	Vermont	78.4
3=	New Hampshire	78.4
5	Connecticut	78.3
6=	California	78.1
6=	Massachusetts	78.1
8=	Colorado	77.8
8=	Washington	77.8
8=	New Jersey	77.8
8=	New York	77.8

Source: Institute for Health Metrics and Evaluation at the University of Washington.

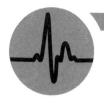

US STATES WITH LOWEST MALE LIFE EXPECTANCY

	State	Male life expectancy (in years)
1	Mississippi	71.8
2=	Arizona	72.5
2=	West Virginia	72.5
4	Louisiana	72.6
5=	Oklahoma	73
5=	Arkansas	73
7	Kentucky	73.3
8	Tennessee	73.5
9	South Carolina	74
10	Missouri	74.8

Source: Institute for Health Metrics and Evaluation at the University of Washington.

EXTINCTION EVENTS

	Event	Proportion of species wiped out
1	**Permian-Triassic Extinction (252 million years ago)** Changing air composition owing to meteorite or volcanic ash.	90–99%
2=	**Cretaceous–Tertiary Extinction (65 million years ago)** Meteorite crash in Mexico. Mammals overtook dinosaurs as dominant species.	75%
2=	**Late Devonian Extinction (374 million years ago)** Changing air composition owing to meteorite or volcanic ash. Among the lost species were forests of fungi 26 ft (8 m) tall.	75%
4	**Triassic–Jurassic Extinction (205 million years ago)** Volcanic ash, changing atmosphere.Lasted only 10,000 years (most extinction-level events last millions of years).	65%
5	**Ordovician-Silurian Extinction (443 million years ago)** A rapid ice age owing to lowered carbon dioxide levels.	Over 60%
6	**End-Ediacaran Extinction (542 million years ago)** Unknown reasons.Some of these creatures form today's fossil fuels.	Over 50%
7	**Cambrian-Ordovician Extinction** **(488 million years ago)** Unknown reasons. A glaciation may have occurred (the coldest part of an ice age)	Over 40% of life wiped out
8	**The Lau Event (420 million years ago)** Sudden climate change, unknown reasons. Many creatures found the new atmospheric gases toxic.	30%
9	**End-Jurassic Extinction (200 million years ago)** Unknown. Mostly aquatic.	20%
10	**Carboniferous Rainforest Collapse** **(305 million years ago)** A brief ice age killed rainforests and lowered carbon dioxide levels.	Almost 10%

Source: Listverse

TOP CAUSES OF DEATH IN THE US*

1   Diseases of heart

2   Malignant neoplasms

3   Chronic lower respiratory diseases

4   Cerebrovascular diseases

5   Accidents (unintentional injuries)

6   Alzheimer's disease

7   Diabetes mellitus

8   Nephritis, nephrotic syndrome, and nephrosis

9   Influenza and pneumonia

10 Intentional self-harm (suicide)

*Per CDC: "[These figures] are based on death records comprising more than 98% of
the demographic and medical files for all deaths in the United States in 2010. The records
are weighted to independent control counts for 2010. Comparisons are made with
2009 final data."
Source: National Vital Statistics Reports

THE 10
LEADING CAUSES OF DEATH WORLDWIDE

	Cause	Deaths in millions	% of deaths
1	Ischaemic heart disease	7.25	12.8
2	Stroke and other cerebrovascular disease	6.15	10.8
3	Lower respiratory infections	3.46	6.1
4	Chronic obstructive pulmonary disease	3.28	5.8
5	Diarrhoeal diseases	2.46	4.3
6	HIV/AIDS	1.78	3.1
7	Trachea, bronchus, lung cancers	1.39	2.4
8	Tuberculosis	1.34	2.4
9	Diabetes mellitus	1.26	2.2
10	Road traffic accidents	1.21	2.1

Source: World Health Organization

DEADLIEST US STATES FOR LAW OFFICERS

	State	Officers killed in 2001–2010
1=	California	50
1=	Texas	45
1=	Florida	28
4	Louisiana	25
5	Pennsylvania	23
6=	Georgia	19
6=	North Carolina	19
6=	Virginia	19
6=	Alabama	19
10	Michigan	18

Source: Federal Bureau of Investigation

THE 10
DEADLIEST US WARS
(BY AMERICAN FATALITIES)

	War	Years	Deaths
1	American Civil War	1861–1865	est. 625,000
2	World War II	1941–1945	405,3996
3	World War I	1917–1918	116,516
4	Vietnam War	1955–1975	58,209
5	Korean War	1950–1953	36,516
6	American Revolutionary War	1775–1783	25,000
7	War of 1812	1812–1815	20,000
8	Mexican–American War	1846–1848	13,283
9	War on Terror*	2001–present	6,280
10	Philippine–American War	1898–1913	4,196

*Afghanistan and Iraq Wars total, as of September 2012

DEADLIEST OCCUPATIONS IN THE USA

	Occupation	Number of fatalities	Rate per 100,000 full-time equivalent workers
1	Fishers and related fishing workers	38	152
2	Logging workers	60	93.5
3	Aircraft pilots and flight engineers	78	70.6
4	Farmers and ranchers	308	42.5
5	Mining machine operators	22	37
6	Roofers	57	32.4
7	Refuse and recyclable material collectors	26	29.8
8	Driver/sales workers and truck drivers	718	23
9	Industrial machinery installation, repair, and maintenance workers	98	20.7
10	Police and sheriff's patrol officers	134	18.1

Source: US Department of Labor

US STATES WITH HIGHEST MORTALITY RATES

	State	Adjusted mortality rate*
1	Mississippi	1,020
2	Louisiana	1,006
3	Alabama	997
4	West Virginia	991
5	Kentucky	975
6	Tennessee	967
7	Oklahoma	966
8	Arkansas	946
9	South Carolina	934
10	Georgia	932

*Deaths per 100,000 people in 2010, adjusted for age of state's population.
If District of Columbia were included, it would be #3, with 1,000.
Source: cdc.gov/nchs and Insider Monkey

US STATES WITH LOWEST MORTALITY

	State	Deaths per 100,000*
1	Hawaii	589.6
2	California	646.8
3	Connecticut	653.5
4	Minnesota	661.4
5	New York	665.4
6	Massachusetts	675.0
7	Colorado	682.7
8	New Hampshire	690.4
9	New Jersey	691.2
10	Washington	692.3

*Age-adjusted rate, which accounts for changes in the age distribution of the population.
(For the USA as a whole, the rate is 746.2 per 100,000 population.)
Source: US Centers for Disease Control and Prevention

COUNTRIES WITH MOST WORK FATALITIES

	Country	Fatalities per 100,000	Total fatalities
1	China	10.5	73,615
2	India	11.5	48,176
3	Indonesia	20.9	18,220
4	Bangladesh	26.4	14,403
5	Brazil	16.6	11,304
6	Vietnam	27.0	9,988
7	Nigeria	20.1	9,631
8	Thailand	23.3	7,490
9	Russia	11.0	6,974
10	USA	5.2	6,821

Source: International Labour Organization of the United Nations

THE 10
DEADLIEST COAL MINE DISASTERS

	Event	Date	Deaths
1	Benxihu colliery explosion, China	1942	1,549
2	Courrières mine disaster, Courrières, France	1906	1,099
3	Mitsubishi Höjö, Kyūshū, Japan	1914	687
4	Laobaidong colliery coal dust explosion, Datong, China	1960	682
5	Mitsui Miike coal mine disaster, Mitsui Miike, Ömuta, Fukuoka, Japan	1963	458
6	Senghenydd colliery disaster, Senghenydd, Wales	1913	439
7	Coalbrook, South Africa	1960	437
8	Wankie coal mine disaster Wankie, Rhodesia/Zimbabwe	1972	426
9	New Yubari, Yūbari, Hokkaidö, Japan	1914	422
10	Bergkamen, West Germany	1946	405

DEADLIEST MARITIME DISASTERS

	Vessel	Location	Year	Deaths
1	MV *Doña Paz*	Tablas Strait, Philippines	1987	1,565–4,400*
2	SS *Kiangya*	Near Shanghai	1948	2,750–3,920‡
3	MV *Joola*	Senegal	2002	1,863
4	SS *Sultana*	Mississippi River	1865	1,547
5	RMS *Titanic*	North Atlantic	1912	1,517
6	RMS *Lusitania*•	off south coast of Ireland	1915	1,195
7	*Toya Maru*	Tsugaru Strait	1954	1,159
8	SS *General Slocum*	New York	1904	1,021
9	MS *al-Salam Boccaccio 98*	Red Sea	2006	1,018
10	RMS *Empress of Ireland*	Saint Lawrence River	1914	1,012

*Estimates vary because of inadequate passenger records.
‡Stowaways on board make it difficult to be exact.
•Torpedoed during World War I

THE 10
DEADLIEST NUCLEAR ACCIDENTS

	Event	Date	Deaths
1	Chernobyl disaster in Ukraine	Apr. 26, 1986	4,056*
2	Mayak nuclear waste storage tank explosion	Sept. 29, 1957	200
3	Windscale fire in the UK‡	Oct. 8, 1957	33
4	Instituto Oncologico Nacional of Panama•	Aug. 2000–Mar. 2001	17
5	Radiotherapy accident in Costa Rica	1996	13
6	Radiotherapy accident in Zaragoza, Spain	Dec. 1990	11
7=	Soviet submarine K-431 accident	Aug. 10, 1985	10
7=	Columbus radiotherapy accident	1974–1976	10
9	Soviet submarine K-27 accident	May 24, 1968	9
10	Soviet submarine K-19 accident	July 4, 1961	8

*56 immediate deaths, plus 4,000 attributed to cancer
‡Plutonium ignited by fire led to radiation exposure.
•Lethal doses of radiation used during cancer treatments

FIRST SPACE EXPLORATION CASUALTIES

	Casualty	Date	Cause
1	Vladimir Komarov	Apr. 24, 1967*	Parachute failure
2=	Georgi Dobrovolski‡	June 30, 1971	Decompression
2=	Viktor Patsayev‡	June 30, 1971	Decompression
2=	Vladislav Volkov‡	June 30, 1971	Decompression
5=	Greg Jarvis	Jan. 28, 1986	*Challenger* explosion
5=	Christa McAuliffe	Jan. 28, 1986	*Challenger* explosion
5=	Ronald McNair	Jan. 28, 1986	*Challenger* explosion
5=	Ellison Onizuka	Jan. 28, 1986	*Challenger* explosion
5=	Judith Resnik	Jan. 28, 1986	*Challenger* explosion
5=	Michael J. Smith	Jan. 28, 1986	*Challenger* explosion
5=	Dick Scobee	Jan. 28, 1986	*Challenger* explosion

*There were several accidents prior to 1967 involving astronauts/pilots in training who were not yet attempting to journey into space.
‡Technically, the only deaths to occur while in outer space

DEADLIEST STAMPEDES/ PANICS

	Event	Location	Year	Death toll
1	Panic at an air raid shelter during Japanese bombing	Chongqing, China	1941	4,000
2	Stampede by pilgrims inside a pedestrian tunnel	Mecca	1990	1,426
3	Khodynka tragedy at coronation of Nicholas II	Moscow	1896	1,389
4	Baghdad bridge stampede	Baghdad, Iraq	2005	953
5	Kumbh Mela stampede	Allahabad, India	1954	800
6	Stampede at the stoning of the devil ritual	Mecca	2006	362
7	Phnom Penh stampede	Phnom Penh, Cambodia	2010	357
8	Stampede at the stoning of the devil ritual	Mecca	1994	270
9	Crowd crush at religious festival	Wai, Maharashtra, India	2005	258
10	Stampede at the stoning of the devil ritual	Mecca	2004	251

DEADLIEST STRUCTURAL COLLAPSES

	Collapsed structure	Location	Year	Deaths
1	Fidenae amphitheatre	near Rome	AD 27	20,000*
2	Upper tier of Circus Maximus	Rome	c. AD 140	1,112
3	Sampoong department store	Seoul, South Korea	1995	502
4	Bleachers at bullring/ stadium	Sincelejo, Colombia.	1980	approx 200
5	Illegally constructed nine-story building	Dhaka, Bangladesh	2005	153
6	Makahali River bridge	Baitadi, Nepal	1974	140
7	Apartment building	Karachi, Pakistan	1976	139
8	Royal Plaza Hotel	Nakhon Ratchasima, Thailand	1993	135
9	Wire rope bridge	Munnar, Kerala, India	1984	125
10	Nuns' school chapel	Biblian, Canar, Ecuador	1963	120

*Estimated figure including dead and wounded

THE 10
MOST DEVASTATING STRUCTURAL FIRES

	Site of fire/location	Year	Deaths
1	Church of the Company in Santiago, Chile	1863	2,000+
2	Theater in Kamli, China	1893	1,995
3	Theater in Canton, China	1845	1,670
4	Theater in Shanghai, China	1871	900
5	Lehman Theater in St. Petersburg, Russia	1836	800
6	Cinema in Xinjiang, China	1977	667
7	Antoung movie theater in China	1937	658
8	Iroquois Theater in Chicago, Illinois	1903	602
9	Theater in Tientsin, China	1872	600
10	Dabwali tent in Haryana, India	1995	540

WORST RAILROAD DISASTERS

	Event	Date/place	Deaths*
1	Sri Lanka tsunami-rail disaster	Sri Lanka, 2004	approx. 1,700
2	Saint-Michel-de-Maurienne derailment	France, 1917	800–1,000
3	Ciurea rail disaster	Romania, 1917	600–1,000
4	Bihar train disaster	India, 1981	500–800
5	Guadalajara train disaster	Mexico, 1915	600+
6	Ufa train disaster	Russia, 1989	575
7	Balvano train disaster	Italy, 1944	521–600+
8	Torre del Bierzo rail disaster	Spain, 1944	200–500+
9	Awash rail disaster	Awash, Afar, Ethiopia, 1985	428
10	Al Ayatt train disaster	Egypt, 2002	383

*Estimated figure

SOLE SURVIVORS OF DEADLIEST AVIATION CRASHES

	Survivor	Flight	Date	Fatalities
1	Cecelia Cichan	Northwest Airlines flight 255	Aug. 16, 1987	154
2	Bahia Bakari	Yemenia flight 626	June 30, 2009	152
3	Bambang Sumadi	Indonesian Air Force	Oct. 5, 1991	136
4	Mohammed el-Fateh Osman	Sudan Airways flight 139	July 8, 2003	116
5	Ruben van Assouw	Afriqiyah Airways flight 771	May 12, 2010	103
6	Youcef Djillali	Air Algérie flight 6289	Mar. 6, 2003	102

7	Juan Loo	LANSA flight 502	Aug. 9, 1970	99
8	Juliane Koepcke	LANSA flight 508	Dec. 24, 1971	91
9	Sergei Petrov	Tajik Air flight 3183	Dec. 15, 1997	85
10	Neil James Campbell	Pan Am flight 8168	July 22, 1973	7

Rade Jevremovich survived the crash of Avioimpex flight 110 in 1993, which killed 115 other people, but he died of his injuries 12 days later.

THE 10
MOST RECENT PIRATES IN US HISTORY*

Name	Territory	Last active year
1 Roaring Dan Seavey	Great Lakes	1920s

Seavey had every 19th-century job one could think of: sailor, saloon owner, Klondike gold prospector ... and pirate, which makes it especially odd that the US Marshals gave him a position—maybe they figured that they could bribe him into pretending to behave. He retired from both crime and crime-fighting by 1930.

2 Bill Johnston	US-Canadian borders	1860

Johnston was a Canadian and a loyal Briton, whose only crime was smuggling. When the War of 1812 began, he was accused of spying, and he lost everything. The false charges became true soon enough, as Johnston became a spy, saboteur, and pirate—though more in the capacity of a privateer. After the war, he went back to smuggling, but was also paid by the US government to spy on Canadian smugglers.

3 John A. Murrell	Mississippi River	1834

Gee, what kind of crimes didn't John Murrell get into? Piracy was just something he did because he ran out of land to break the law upon. Some of his outlaw behavior even contradicted his other crimes. He was purportedly behind some slave uprisings (that's good) but he also kidnapped slaves (that's bad) to sell elsewhere.

4 James Ford	Ohio River area	1833

This one's straight out of a Gary Cooper movie—James Ford was the most respected man in town: wealthy, well liked, and a major in the Illinois militia. However, an easy life wasn't enough for Ford, who became a river pirate, plundering the region he already controlled.

5 Charles Gibbs	Caribbean	1831

Charles Gibbs had the unwanted honor of being one of the last folks ever executed for piracy in the USA. He was involved in at least two mutinies, and plenty of piracy/privateering. Much of his life is obscure, but he had a reputation as being astoundingly cruel.

6   Col. "Plug" Fluger   Ohio River area   1820

With a name like "The Last of the Boat-Wreckers," you're either a pirate or an iceberg. According to newspaper accounts of the era, he was a born conman, thief, hustler, grifter, and all-around awful person. He drowned in a squall, clutching a barrel of whiskey, like pirates do.

7   The Harpe Brothers   rivers of the   1804 (Wiley)/
                            Midwest and South   1799 (Micajah)

Also known as "America's First Serial Killers," they were born to Scottish immigrants in North Carolina. They spent the Revolutionary War fighting for the Tories. Their lives and names are shrouded in mystery, but what isn't in doubt is that they were utter brutes who thrived on blood and theft. When they were finally captured and killed, they had at least 40 lives to account for.

8   Peter Alston   Mississippi River   1804

When your dad's a counterfeiter, you have to work extra hard to impress him with just how much you can infuriate the federal government. Alston really took it to that extra level when he beheaded his own partner in crime to claim the reward (see Samuel Mason, below).

9   Samuel Mason   Mississippi River   1803

Here's a tip: If you're going to flee the charges against you, don't carry 20 human scalps and $7,000 in cash in your bag. When Mason broke out of captivity he was killed either by guards or by his own pirates. Two of the latter (Alston and Wiley Harpe) brought his head in to claim the bounty on it—only to be recognized, arrested, and killed.

10   Alexander White   US eastern seaboard   1784

Scant details about White are available, but we do know that he was hanged for piracy in Cambridge, Massachusetts.

*Pirates of American origin and operations only (Bill Johnston being a borderline case). If he is removed from the list, Frenchman Jean LaFitte qualifies. Active in the Gulf of Mexico in the early 19th century, he was wanted by the US government but also ended up fighting on its behalf.

MOST DANGEROUS SPORTS IN THE USA

	Sport	Injuries per year*
1	Basketball	2,560,000
2	Bicycling	2,490,000
3	Football	2,380,000
4	Softball	1,000,000
5	Baseball	763,000
6	Skateboarding	676,000
7	Horseback riding	316,000
8	Golf	127,000
9	Ice hockey	105,000
10	Lacrosse	96,000

*Based on the estimated number of injuries per year, rather than the percentage of participants who are injured.
Source: CPSC

INEXPLICABLE SPORTS NICKNAMES

Nickname	Athlete	Sport

1   The Boston Strangler   Andrew Toney   Basketball
Toney's ability to shut down the Celtics earned him this callous nickname.

2   Pork Chop   Clyde Pough   Baseball
When a Little League team in the '80s had two kids nicknamed Pokey, Li'l Pough's moniker was changed to "Pork Chop" to avoid confusion.

3   Dr. Dunkenstein   Darrell Griffith   Basketball
The only careers in which this isn't a great nickname are lifeguard and obstetrician, but it makes less sense as you think about it. One can't assemble a dunk from parts of other shots.

4   Lord of the Ring-Dings   Jared Lorenzen   Football
At 285 lbs, Lorenzen is twice the size of most quarterbacks, but other nicknames at least reference his skill (e.g. The Pillsbury Throwboy). This is just a fat joke.

5   Old Poison   Nels Stewart   Hockey
Stewart got this nickname for his efficacy on the ice, but it's the "Old" that makes this odd, considering he'd retired a champ by age 36.

6   Linford's Lunchbox   Linford Christie   Track & Field
This UK sprinter found his genitalia the focus of unwanted scrutiny when the press noticed how form-fitting his track suit was.

7   Tubesteak   Terry Tracy   Surfing
Not another crotch joke, this pseudonym was either because he worked at Tube's Steak & Lobster House, or for showing off. Still, guys … still.

8   Jesus Shuttlesworth   Ray Allen   Basketball
Acting commendably in Spike Lee's *He Got Game* earned Allen his character's name.

9   The Dancing Bear   Ron McDole   Football
Plenty of ways for a defensive end to get a nickname like this, involving interceptions and playing for Chicago, but not embarrassing dance steps at a nightclub.

10   The Great Poohdini   Derrick Rose   Football
When Rose was a baby, his grandma said he looked like Winnie the Pooh. Awww. Wait…how did this morph into a Houdini portmanteau twenty years on?

LARGEST* ATHLETES' HEARTS

1   Tour de France cyclists
2   Marathon runners
3   Rowers
4   Boxers
5   Sprint cyclists
6   Middle-distance runners
7   Weightlifters
8   Swimmers
9   Sprinters
10 Decathletes

*Based on average medical measurements

TOP FEMALE BADMINTON PLAYERS IN 2012*

1   Wang Yihan

2   Li Xuerui

3   Wang Xin

4   Saina Nehwal

5   Wang Shixian

6   Juliane Schenk

7   Tine Baun

8   Sung Ji Hyun

9   Jiang Yanjiao

10   Ratchanok Intanon

*As of November 26, 2012
Source: Badminton World Federation

TOP MALE BADMINTON PLAYERS IN 2012*

1   Lin Dan

2   Lee Chong Wei

3   Chen Long

4   Chen Jin

5   Peter Hoeg Gade

6   Simon Santoso

7   Sho Sasaki

8   Lee Hyun Il

9   Kenichi Tago

10   Du Pengyu

*As of November 26, 2012
Source: Badminton World Federation

WORLD'S LARGEST RUNNING EVENTS

	Race	Location	Date	Participants
1	Kahit Isang Araw Lang Unity Run	Philippines	Jan. 22, 2012	209,000
2	A Run for the Pasig River	Philippines	Oct. 10, 2010	116,086
3	Bay to Breakers	San Francisco, CA	May 18, 1986	110,000
4	Cursa El Corte Ingles	Barcelona, Spain	June 5, 1994	109,457
5	Broloppet	Amager, Denmark, to Malmö, Sweden via Øresund Bridge	June 12, 2000	92,266
6	City2Surf	Sydney, Australia	Aug. 14, 2011	86,696
7	JP Morgan Chase Corporate Challenge	Frankfurt, Germany	June 11, 2008	73,719
8	Lilac Bloomsday Run	Spokane, WA	May 5, 1996	61,298
9=	United We Run	Beirut, Lebanon	Apr. 10, 2005	60,000
9=	Vancouver Sun Run	Vancouver, B.C., Canada	Apr. 15, 2012	60,000

MOST APPEARANCES IN A WWE ROYAL RUMBLE

	Wrestler	WWE (World Wrestling Entertainment) royal rumbles entered	First rumble	Most recent rumble
1	Kane*	15	1996	2011
2	Shawn Michaels	12	1989	2010
3=	Rikishi‡	10	1993	2004
3=	The Undertaker	10	1991	2009
5=	Big Show	9	2000	2012
5=	Big Daddy V•	9	1994	2008
7=	Triple H**	8	1996	2010
7=	Shelton Benjamin	8	2003	2010
7=	Booker T‡‡	8	2002	2012
10	Billy Gunn	7	1994	2004

*Including his previous personas, Isaac Yankem and the new Diesel

‡Including his previous personas, Fatu and the Sultan

•Including his previous personas, Mabel and Viscera

**Including his previous persona, Hunter Hearst Helmsley

‡‡Including his previous persona, King Booker

GREATEST SPORTS MOVIES

1   Rocky
The original is still the best.

2   Hoosiers
This movie is notable for numerous reasons, but none more so than it showcases a basketball team from South Bend that was actually favored.

3   Field of Dreams
If you're not moved by James Earl Jones' monologue on the history of the game then there may not be any joy for you in this world.

4   Rudy
This beautifully-scored movie showcases a determined-yet-undersized Sean Astin overcoming impossible challenges before him.

5   A League of Their Own
Just because this book is for men, that doesn't mean we can't enjoy the hell out of a movie about the All-American Girl's Professional Baseball League.

6   The Replacements
See? We're a sucker for Gene Hackman playing a disgruntled coach.

7   Moneyball
Some of the movies on this list are designed for the casual fan to pick up, cheer for the "everyman" for 90 minutes, and then move on feeling pretty good. We think Moneyball demands a little love of the game beforehand.

8   Rocky IV
Easily the campiest of the Rocky series, it's also a total guilty pleasure.

9   The Sandlot
Funny, touching, heartwarming, and exciting, all in the same stroke.

10 Remember the Titans
We always get a kick out of Ethan Suplee.

TOP FANTASY FOOTBALL PERFORMANCES EVER

	Player	Team	Fantasy points
1	Clinton Portis	Washington Redskins	54
2	Shaun Alexander	Seattle Seahawks	52
3	Doug Martin	Tampa Bay Buccaneers	51
4=	Michael Vick	Philadelphia Eagles	49
4=	Mike Anderson	Denver Broncos	49
6=	Fred Taylor	Jacksonville Jaguars	48
6=	Priest Holmes	Kansas City Chiefs	48
8=	Jimmy Smith	Jacksonville Jaguars	47
8=	Marshall Faulk	St. Louis Rams	47
8=	Jerome Harrison	Cleveland Browns	47

Source: Sports.espn.go.com

QUARTERBACKS WITH THE MOST PASSING YARDS

	Player	Yards	Year
1	Drew Brees	5,476	2011
2	Tom Brady	5,235	2011
3	Drew Brees	5,177	2012
4	Dan Marino	5,084	1984
5	Drew Brees	5,069	2008
6	Matthew Stafford	5,038	2011
7	Matthew Stafford	4,967	2012
8	Eli Manning	4,933	2011
9	Tony Romo	4,903	2012
10	Kurt Warner	4,830	2001

Source: Pro-football-reference.com
This list was compiled at the end of the 2012 season.

BEST SINGLE-GAME PASSING YARDAGE

	Player	Yards (meters)	Year
1	Norm Van Brocklin	554 yd (506.6 m)	1951
2	Warren Moon	527 yd (481.9 m)	1990
3	Boomer Esiason	522 yd (477.3 m)	1996
4	Dan Marino	521 yd (476.4 m)	1988
5	Matthew Stafford	520 yd (475.4 m)	2012
6	Tom Brady	517 yd (472.7 m)	2011
7	Phil Simms	513 yd (469.1 m)	1985
8=	Drew Brees	510 yd (466.3 m)	2006
8=	Eli Manning	510 yd (466.3 m)	2012
10	Vince Ferragamo	509 yd (465.4 m)	1982

Source: Pro-football-reference.com

MOST RECENTLY DEFUNCT NFL TEAMS

	Team	Final year of play
1	Dallas Texans	1952*
2	New York Yanks	1951‡
3	Baltimore Colts	1950
4	Brooklyn Tigers	1944•
5	Cincinnati Reds	1934
6	St. Louis Gunners	1934
7	Cleveland Indians	1931
8	Toledo Maroons	1923
9	Youngstown Patricians	1922**
10	Syracuse Pros	1921

*Ted Collins could not hold on to a team.
‡Another Collins team, rapidly changing names and cities
•Folded into the Boston Yanks
**Joined league, never played

NFL CAREER SACKS LEADERS

	Player	Sacks	Years active
1	Bruce Smith	200.0	1985–2003
2	Reggie White	198.0	1985–2000
3	Kevin Greene	160.0	1985–1999
4	Chris Doleman	150.5	1985–1999
5	Michael Strahan	141.5	1993–2007
6	Jason Taylor	139.5	1997–2011
7=	Richard Dent	137.5	1983–1997
7=	John Randle	137.5	1990–2003
9=	Lawrence Taylor	132.5	1981–1993
9=	Leslie O'Neal	132.5	1986–1999

Source: Pro-football-reference.com

NFL SINGLE-SEASON SACKS LEADERS

	Player	Sacks	Year	Team
1	Michael Strahan	22.5*	2001	New York Giants
2	Jared Allen	22.0	2011	Minnesota Vikings
3	Mark Gastineau	22.0	1984	New York Jets
4=	Chris Doleman	21.0	1989	Minnesota Vikings
4=	Reggie White	21.0	1987	Philadelphia Eagles
7=	Lawrence Taylor	20.5*	1986	New York Giants
7=	J.J. Watt	20.5*	2012	Houston Texans
9=	Derrick Thomas	20.0	1990	Kansas City Chiefs
9=	DeMarcus Ware	20.0	2008	Dallas Cowboys
11=	Tim Harris	19.5*	1989	Green Bay Packers
11=	DeMarcus Ware	19.5*	2011	Dallas Cowboys

*A half sack is awarded any time multiple players are responsible for the sack. Interestingly, this is even true if more than two players sack the quarterback. In other words, if five players all got to the quarterback at once, they would all receive credit for half a sack.
Source: Pro-football-reference.com

NFL CAREER INTERCEPTIONS LEADERS

	Player	Interceptions	Years active
1	Paul Krause	81	1964–1979
2	Emlen Tunnell	79	1948–1961
3	Rod Woodson	71	1987–2003
4	Dick "Night Train" Lane	68	1952–1965
5	Ken Riley	65	1969–1983
6=	Darren Sharper	63	1997–2010
6=	Ronnie Lott	63	1981–1994
8=	Dave Brown	62	1975–1989
8=	Dick LeBeau	62	1959–1972
10	Emmitt Thomas	58	1966–1978

Source: Pro-football-reference.com

TOP 10

NFL SINGLE-SEASON INTERCEPTIONS LEADERS

	Player	Interceptions	Year	Team
1	Dick "Night Train" Lane	14	1952	Los Angeles Rams
2=	Lester Hayes	13	1980	Oakland Raiders
2=	Spec Sanders	13	1950	New York Yanks
2=	Dan Sandifer	13	1948	Washington Redskins
5=	Emmitt Thomas	12	1974	Kansas City Chiefs
5=	Paul Krause	12	1964	Washington Redskins
5=	Bob Nussbaumer	12	1949	Chicago Cardinals
5=	Jack Christiansen	12	1953	Detroit Lions
5=	Don Doll	12	1950	Detroit Lions
5=	Woodley Lewis	12	1950	Los Angeles Rams
5=	Dainard Paulson	12	1964	New York Jets
5=	Mike Reinfeldt	12	1979	Houston Oilers
5=	Fred Glick	12	1963	Houston Oilers

Source: Pro-football-reference.com

NCAA COACHES WITH THE HIGHEST WIN-LOSS PERCENTAGE

Coach		Win %	School
1	Knute Rockne	.8811	Notre Dame
2	Frank Leahy	.8643	Boston College, Notre Dame
3	Barry Switzer	.8368	Oklahoma
4	Tom Osborne	.8355	Nebraska
5	Urban Meyer	.8345	Bowling Green State, Utah, Florida, Ohio State
6	Charley Moran	.8333	Texas A&M, Centre
6	Fielding Yost	.8333	Michigan
8	Bob Neyland	.8287	Tennessee
9	Jim Tressel*	.8281	Ohio State
10	Bud Wilkinson	.8258	Oklahoma

*The record for Jim Tressel has been adjusted to 94 wins—21 losses by the NCAA
Minimum of 10 Years Coaching
Source: www.sports-reference.com

COLLEGES WITH MOST HEISMAN TROPHY WINNERS

	Team	Number of Heisman winners
1	Notre Dame	7
2	Ohio State	7*
3	USC	6‡
4	Oklahoma	5
5=	Army	3
5=	Florida	3
5=	Michigan	3
5=	Nebraska	3
5=	Auburn	3
6=	Florida State, Georgia, Miami, Navy, Texas, Wisconsin, Yale	2

*Ohio State has won the trophy seven times, but had only six winners, as Archie Griffin won twice.
‡USC had seven, until Reggie Bush returned his 2005 Heisman.
This list was compiled up to the beginning of the 2012 season.
Source: Heisman

INAUGURAL LINGERIE FOOTBALL LEAGUE TEAMS

	Team	Location of inaugural game
1	Chicago Bliss	Sears Centre (Hoffman Estates, IL)
2	Miami Caliente	BankAtlantic Center (Sunrise, FL)
3	New York Majesty	Sovereign Center (Reading, PA)
4	Philadelphia Passion	Sun National Bank Center (Trenton, NJ)
5	Tampa Breeze	Tampa Bay Times Forum (St. Pete) (Tampa, FL)
6	Dallas Desire	QuikTrip Park (Grand Prairie, TX)
7	Denver Dream	Dick's Sporting Goods Park (Commerce City, CO)
8	Los Angeles Temptation	Los Angeles Memorial Sports Arena (Los Angeles, CA)
9	San Diego Seduction	San Diego Sports Arena (San Diego, CA)
10	Seattle Mist	ShoWare Center (Kent, WA)

THE 10
BEST VIDEO GAME ATHLETES

	Athlete	Game
1	Bo Jackson	Tecmo Super Bowl
2	Jeremy Roenick	NHL '94
3	Michael Vick	Madden 2001
4	Lefty	Baseball Stars
5	Fat Hockey Player	Ice Hockey
6	Barry Sanders	Tecmo Super Bowl
7	Chris Mullin	NBA Jam
8	Little Mac	Mike Tyson's Punch-Out!!
9	Tommy Haas	Virtua Tennis
10	Randy Moss	NFL 2K1

TOP 10

TEAMS WITH MOST SUPER BOWL WINS

	Team	Wins
1	Pittsburgh Steelers	6
2=	San Francisco 49ers	5
2=	Dallas Cowboys	5
4=	Green Bay Packers	4
4=	New York Giants	4
6=	Oakland (LA) Raiders	3
6=	Washington Redskins	3
6=	New England Patriots	3
9=	Baltimore/Indianapolis Colts	2
9=	Miami Dolphins	2
9=	Denver Broncos	2

MOST HOME RUNS IN A SINGLE YEAR

	Player	Home runs	Year
1	Bobby Abreu	41	2005
2	Josh Hamilton	35	2008
3=	David Ortiz	32	2010
3=	Robinson Cano	32	2011
5	Adrian Gonzalez	31	2011
6	Prince Fielder	28	2012
7	Miguel Tejada	27	2004
8=	Sammy Sosa	26	2000
8=	Albert Pujols	26	2003
8=	Hanley Ramirez	26	2010

Source: Baseball Almanac

TOP 10
BEST LIFETIME BATTING AVERAGES

	Player	Batting average*
1	Ty Cobb	.366 (.36636)
2	Rogers Hornsby	.358 (.35850)
3	Joe Jackson	.356 (.35575)
4	Pete Browning	.349 (.34892)
5	Ed Delahanty	.346 (.34590)
6	Tris Speaker	.345 (.34468)
7	Ted Williams	.344 (.34441)
8	Billy Hamilton	.344 (.34429)
9	Dan Brouthers	.342 (.34212)
10	Babe Ruth	.342 (.34206)

*Minimum 1,000 career games played and at-bats
Source: Baseball Almanac

BEST SINGLE-SEASON BATTING AVERAGES

	Player	Average	Year	Team	League
1	Tip O'Neill	.485 (.48501)*	1887	St. Louis Browns	AA
2	Pete Browning	.457 (.45681)*	1887	Louisville Colonels	AA
3	Bob Caruthers	.456 (.45581)*	1887	St. Louis Browns	AA
4	Hugh Duffy	.440 (.43970)	1894	Boston Beaneaters	NL
5	Ross Barnes	.429 (.42857)	1876	Chicago White Stockings	NL
6	Yank Robinson	.427 (.42720)	1887	St. Louis Browns	AA
7	Willie Keeler	.424 (.42376)	1897	Baltimore Orioles	NL
8	Rogers Hornsby	.424 (.42351)	1924	St. Louis Cardinals	NL
9	Nap Lajoie	.421 (.42096)	1901	Philadelphia Athletics	AL
10	George Sisler	.420 (.41980)	1922	St. Louis Browns	AL

*In 1887, when a player was walked, it was officially counted as a "hit." As a result, these numbers may appear higher than usual.
Source: Baseball Almanac

ALL-TIME BEST EARNED RUN AVERAGES

	Pitcher*	ERA
1	Ed Walsh	1.82 (1.816)
2	Addie Joss	1.89 (1.887)
3	Jim Devlin	1.89 (1.890)
4	Jack Pfiester	2.02 (2.024)
5	Joe Wood	2.03 (2.030)
6	Mordecai Brown	2.06 (2.057)
7	John Ward	2.10 (2.102)
8	Christy Mathewson	2.13 (2.133)
9	Rube Waddell	2.16 (2.161)
10	Walter Johnson	2.17 (2.167)

*Mariano Rivera would be #11 on this list, with a 2.21 ERA. He sat out the 2012 season and, as of September 2012, the future of his career is unknown.
Source: Baseball Almanac

MOST MLB ALL-STAR GAME APPEARANCES

	Player	All-Star games
1	Hank Aaron	21
2=	Willie Mays	20
2=	Stan Musial	20
4	Cal Ripken	19
5=	Rod Carew	18
5=	Carl Yastrzemski	18
7=	Ted Williams	17
7=	Pete Rose	17
9	Mickey Mantle	16
10=	Yogi Berra	15
10=	Al Kaline	15
10=	Brooks Robinson	15
10=	Tony Gwynn	15
10=	Ozzie Smith	15

*Major League Baseball
Source: baseball-reference.com

BEST SINGLE-SEASON EARNED RUN AVERAGES

	Player	ERA	Year	Team	League
1	Tim Keefe	.86 (.857)	1880	Troy Trojans	NL
2	Dutch Leonard	.96 (.961)	1914	Boston Red Sox	AL
3	Ed Cushman	1.00 (1.000)	1884	Milwaukee Grays	UA
4	Mordecai Brown	1.04 (1.038)	1906	Chicago Cubs	NL
5	Bob Gibson	1.12 (1.123)	1968	St. Louis Cardinals	NL
6	Christy Mathewson	1.14 (1.144)	1909	New York Giants	NL
7	Walter Johnson	1.14 (1.145)	1913	Washington Senators	AL
8	Jack Pfiester	1.15 (1.154)	1907	Chicago Cubs	NL
9	Addie Joss	1.16 (1.163)	1908	Cleveland Naps	AL
10	Carl Lundgren	1.17 (1.174)	1907	Chicago Cubs	NL

Source: Baseball Almanac

TEAMS WITH THE MOST WORLD SERIES WINS

	Team	Championships
1	New York Yankees	27
2	St. Louis Cardinals	11
3	Oakland Athletics	9
4=	Boston Red Sox	7
4=	San Francisco Giants	7
6	Los Angeles Dodgers	6
7=	Cincinnati Reds	5
7=	Pittsburgh Pirates	5
8	Detroit Tigers	4
9=	Baltimore Orioles	3
9=	Chicago White Sox	3
9=	Atlanta Braves	3
9=	Minnesota Twins	3

* Among Active Franchises
As of Spring 2013
Source: www.baseball-reference.com

TOP 10

TEAMS WINNING THE MOST NBA* CHAMPIONSHIPS

	Team	Championships
1	Boston Celtics	17
2	Los Angeles Lakers	16
3	Chicago Bulls	6
4	San Antonio Spurs	4
5=	Detroit Pistons	3
5=	Golden State Warriors (two as the Philadelphia Warriors)	3
5=	Philadelphia 76ers (one as the Syracuse Nationals)	3
8=	Houston Rockets	2
8=	Miami Heat	2
8=	New York Knicks	2

*National Basketball Association
Source: NBA Universe (nbauniverse.com)

UNBREAKABLE WILT CHAMBERLAIN RECORDS

1   100 points in a game

2   Most points per game in a season (50.4)

3   Most points in a season (4,029)*

4   Most rebounds in a season (2,149)

5   Most points in a half (59)

6   Most 50 point games in a season (45)

7   Most 40 point games in a season (45)

8   Most career regular-season 60 point games (32)

9   Most consecutive 50 point games (7)

10   Most consecutive 40 point games (14)

*Only player to break the 4,000 point barrier. The only other player to break the 3,000 barrier is Michael Jordan.

The 7 ft 1 in (216 cm) Chamberlain was the greatest center ever to play basketball. He played for the University of Kansas and the Harlem Globetrotters and then, from 1959 till 1973, for the Philadelphia/San Francisco Warriors, the Philadelphia 76ers, and the Los Angeles Lakers. He was the holder of many records still unbroken. These represent his most ironclad achievements.

Source: NBA Universe (nbauniverse.com)

SHORTEST PLAYERS IN NBA* HISTORY

	Player	Height
1	Tyrone "Muggsy" Bogues	5 ft 3 in (1.6 m)
2	Earl Boykins	5 ft 5 in (1.65 m)
3	Mel Hirsch	5 ft 6 in (1.68 m)
4=	Greg Grant	5 ft 7 in (1.7 m)
4=	Keith Jennings	5 ft 7 in (1.7 m)
4=	Herm Klotz	5 ft 7 in (1.7 m)
4=	Wat Misaka	5 ft 7 in (1.7 m)
4=	Monte Towe	5 ft 7 in (1.7 m)
4=	Spud Webb	5 ft 7 in (1.7 m)
10	Charlie Criss	5 ft 8 in (1.73 m)

*National Basketball Association

MOST RECENTLY DEFUNCT NHL* TEAMS

	Team	Years in existence	Became
1	Atlanta Thrashers	1999–2011	Winnipeg Jets
2	Hartford Whalers	1979–1997	Carolina Hurricanes
3	Winnipeg Jets	1979–1996	Phoenix Coyotes
4	Quebec Nordiques	1979–1995	Colorado Avalanche
5	Minnesota North Stars	1967–1993	Dallas Stars
6	Colorado Rockies	1976–1982	New Jersey Devils
7	Atlanta Flames	1972–1980	Calgary Flames
8	Cleveland Barons	1976–1978	Minnesota North Stars (merger)
9=	California Golden Seals	1967–1976	Cleveland Barons
9=	Kansas City Scouts	1974–1976	Colorado Rockies

*National Hockey League
Source: Hockey-reference.com

TEAMS WITH MOST STANLEY CUP WINS

	Team	Championships
1	Montreal Canadiens	23
2	Toronto Maple Leafs	13
3	Detroit Red Wings	11
4	Boston Bruins	6
5	Edmonton Oilers	5
6	Chicago Blackhawks	4
6	New York Rangers	4
6	New York Islanders	4
9	Pittsburgh Penguins	3
9	New Jersey Devils	3

*Among Active Franchises
As of Spring 2013
Source: www.hockey-reference.com

WOMEN WITH MOST GRAND SLAM TITLES

	Player	Grand Slam wins
1	Margaret Court	24
2	Steffi Graf	22
3	Helen Wills Moody	19
4=	Chris Evert	18
4=	Martina Navratilova	18
6	Serena Williams	15
7	Billie Jean King	12
8=	Maureen Connolly Brinker	9
8=	Monica Seles	9
10	Suzanne Lenglen	8

MEN WITH MOST GRAND SLAM TITLES

	Player	Grand Slam wins
1	Roger Federer	17
2	Pete Sampras	14
3	Roy Emerson	12
4=	Björn Borg	11
4=	Rafael Nadal	11
4=	Rod Laver	11
7	Bill Tilden	10
8=	Ken Rosewall	8
8=	Fred Perry	8
8=	Jimmy Connors	8
8=	Ivan Lendl	8
8=	Andre Agassi	8

MEN WITH MOST WINS IN THE PGA* MAJORS

	Player	Country	Wins	Winning span
1	Jack Nicklaus	USA	18	1962–1986
2	Tiger Woods	USA	14	1996–2012
3	Walter Hagen	USA	11	1914–1936
4=	Gary Player	South Africa	9	1958–1978
4=	Ben Hogan	USA	9	1938–1959
6	Tom Watson	USA	8	1974–1998
7=	Arnold Palmer	USA	7	1955–1973
7=	Sam Snead	USA	7	1936–1965
7=	Gene Sarazen	USA	7	1922–1941
7=	Bobby Jones	USA	7	1923–1930

*Professional Golf Association
Source: tigerwoods.com

GOLFERS WITH BIGGEST MARGINS OF VICTORY

	Player Name	Year	Number of shots	Finishing score
1	Tiger Woods	1997	12	-18
2	Jack Nicklaus	1963	9	-17
3	Raymond Floyd	1976	8	-17
4	Cary Middlecoff	1955	7	-9
5	Arnold Palmer	1964	6	-12
= 6	Ben Hogan	1953	5	-14
= 6	Nick Faldo	1996	5	-12
= 8	Jimmy Demaret	1940	4	-8
= 8	Sam Snead	1949	4	-2
= 8	Seve Ballesteros	1980	4	-13
= 8	Seve Ballesteros	1983	4	-8
= 8	Bernhard Langer	1993	4	-11

Nationalities

USA
Jimmy Demaret, Tiger Woods, Jack Nicklaus, Raymond Floyd, Cary Middlecoff
Arnold Palmer, Ben Hogan, Sam Snead

UK
Nick Faldo

SPAIN
Seve Ballesteros

WOMEN WITH MOST WINS IN THE LPGA* MAJORS

	Player	Country	Wins	Winning span
1	Patty Berg	USA	15	1937–1958
2	Mickey Wright	USA	13	1958–1966
3	Louise Suggs	USA	11	1946–1959
4=	Annika Sörenstam	Sweden	10	1995–2006
4=	Babe Zaharias	USA	10	1940–1954
6	Betsy Rawls	USA	8	1951–1969
7=	Juli Inkster	USA	7	1984–2002
7=	Karrie Webb	Australia	7	1999–2006
9=	Pat Bradley	USA	6	1980–1986
9=	Betsy King	USA	6	1987–1997
9=	Patty Sheehan	USA	6	1983–1996

*Ladies Professional Golf Association

REASONS GOLF IS LOSING POPULARITY

1   It takes a ridiculous amount of lawn maintenance.

2   The rich are consolidating the country's wealth, so there are fewer rich people to play golf.

3   RELATED: It costs a lot of money. Money better spent on beer.

4   There's no running, so its practitioners don't get their cardio in.

5   It has never been exciting on TV.

6   It has never been exciting on a video game.

7   It's a game where a 74-year-old-man can beat a dozen 20-somethings.

8   All those sunny, rollicking hills and you're not allowed to roll down them, as you did when you were young.

9   It's too much like being Scottish.

10   ...and not enough like Halo.

MOST TITLES WON ON A PGA TOUR

	Player	Country	Wins
1	Hale Irwin	USA	45
2	Lee Trevino	USA	29
3	Gil Morgan	USA	25
4	Miller Barber	USA	24
5	Bob Charles	New Zealand	23
6=	Don January	USA	22
6=	Chi-Chi Rodríguez	USA	22
8=	Jim Colbert	USA	20
8=	Bruce Crampton	Australia	20
10=	George Archer	USA	19
10=	Larry Nelson	USA	19
10=	Gary Player	South Africa	19

TEAMS WITH FEWEST MEDALS IN THE SUMMER OLYMPICS

	Team (IOC code)	No. of years Participating	Gold	Silver	Bronze	Total
1	Liechtenstein (LIE)	16	0	0	0	0
2	Bermuda (BER)	17	0	0	1	1
3	Guyana (GUY)	16	0	0	1	1
4	Iraq (IRQ)	13	0	0	1	1
5=	Barbados (BAR)	11	0	0	1	1
5=	Niger (NIG)	11	0	0	1	1
7	Togo (TOG)	9	0	0	1	1
8=	Bahrain (BRN)	8	0	0	1	1
8=	Djibouti (DJI)	8	0	0	1	1
8=	Mauritius (MRI)	8	0	0	1	1

Ranked by total medals per number of years participating.

MOST FREQUENT WINTER OLYMPIC ENTRANTS TO HAVE WON NO MEDALS

	Team (IOC code)	No. of years participating
1=	Argentina (ARG)	17
1=	Greece (GRE)	17
3	Iceland (ISL)	16
4=	Lebanon (LIB)	15
4=	Chile (CHI)	15
4=	Turkey (TUR)	15
7	Mongolia (MGL)	12
8	Chinese Taipei (TPE)	10
9=	Cyprus (CYP)	9
9=	Iran (IRI)	9

Many nations don't compete in the Winter Olympics, but of those who do, these are the most frequent entrants who have yet to win a medal.

NATIONS WINNING MOST MEDALS IN THE SUMMER OLYMPICS

	Country	Gold	Silver	Bronze	Total
1	USA	975	759	667	2,401
2	Soviet Union	395	319	296	1,010
3	Great Britain	236	272	272	780
4	France	202	223	246	671
5	Germany	174	182	217	573
6	Italy	198	166	185	549
7	Sweden	143	164	176	483
8	Hungary	167	144	164	475
9	China	201	144	128	473
10	Australia	138	153	177	468

NATIONS WINNING MOST MEDALS IN THE WINTER OLYMPICS

	Country	Gold	Silver	Bronze	Total
1	Norway	107	106	90	303
2	USA	87	95	71	253
3	Austria	55	70	76	201
4	Soviet Union	78	57	59	194
5	Germany	70	72	48	190
6	Finland	41	59	56	156
7	Canada	52	45	48	145
8	Sweden	48	33	48	129
9	Switzerland	44	37	46	127
10	East Germany	39	36	35	110

NATIONS WITH MOST WINS IN THE SUMMER PARALYMPICS

	Team	Participated	Gold	Silver	Bronze	Total
1	USA	14	697	615	627	1,939
2	Great Britain	14	529	517	511	1,557
3	Germany	14	451	451	421	1,323
4	Canada	12	347	289	311	947
5	Australia	14	339	357	317	1,013
6	China	8	335	259	200	794
7	France	14	302	315	304	921
8	Netherlands	14	247	214	191	652
9	Poland	12	223	216	187	626
10	Spain	12	203	206	221	630

MOST DECORATED OLYMPIANS

	Athlete/Nation	Sport	Years	Total
1	Michael Phelps (USA)	Swimming	2004–2012	22
2	Larisa Latynina (Soviet Union)	Gymnastics	1956–1964	18
3	Nikolai Andrianov (Soviet Union)	Gymnastics	1972–1980	15
4	Boris Shakhlin (Soviet Union)	Gymnastics	1956–1964	13
5	Edoardo Mangiarotti (Italy)	Fencing	1936–1960	13
6	Takashi Ono (Japan)	Gymnastics	1952–1964	13
7	Paavo Nurmi (Finland)	Athletics	1920–1928	12
8=	Birgit Fischer (Germany)	Canoeing	1980–2004	12
8=	Bjørn Dæhlie (Norway)	Cross-country skiing	1992–1998	12
9=	Sawao Kato (Japan)	Gymnastics	1968–1976	12
9=	Jenny Thompson (USA)	Swimming	1992–2004	12

MULTI-SPORT ATHLETES

These rankings are entirely subjective. We tried to compile them based on notable athletes who perform professionally at a very high level. Any omissions are due to the personal opinions of the authors.

1 Jim Thorpe

The undisputed champion, Jim Thorpe played for many teams during his career, including the Cleveland Indians (football), Oorang Indians, Rock Island Independents, New York Giants (football), Chicago Cardinals, New York Giants (baseball), Cincinnati Reds, and Boston Braves. He also won an Olympic gold medal in the Pentathlon *and* the Decathlon.

2 Babe Didrikson Zaharias

Babe Didrikson Zaharias has golf records that stand to this day. She played against men in the Los Angeles Open in 1938. She won every major golf title available, an Olympic gold medal in the 80-meter hurdles, a gold in the javelin throw, and a silver in the high jump. She was also an accomplished basketball player as well as a pool player.

3 "Bullet" Bob Hayes

While many athletes on this list simply played in multiple sports, "Bullet" Bob Hayes *excelled* in multiple sports. Inducted in the Pro Football Hall of Fame, Hayes was a versatile offensive weapon for the Dallas Cowboys, racking up a number of franchise records. When he wasn't playing football, Bob Hayes was setting a world record in the 1964 Olympic Games (with borrowed spikes), not to mention winning two gold medals.

4 Wilt Chamberlain

Chamberlain so thoroughly dominated the game of basketball that he could merely be a hobbyist in a sport and still get his name on this list. Instead, after his basketball career was over, Chamberlain took up volleyball, becoming an MVP-caliber player and an inductee into the Volleyball Hall of Fame.

5 Deion Sanders

Although Sanders's football career was more remarkable than his baseball career—he is considered to be one of the best players ever to play the game, an eight-time Pro Bowler and a two-time Super Bowl champion, as well as the recipient of the Jim Thorpe award—his baseball career was not without merit. Sanders remains the only player to appear in both a World Series and a Super Bowl.

6 Bo Jackson

Jackson had the potential to be a once-in-a-lifetime player in both football and baseball. An injury ended his career prematurely, but in his four short years he amassed some impressive accomplishments, including a 221-yard rushing performance on Monday Night Football. In baseball, he had an All Star Game selection and an All Star Game MVP award, plus four 20 home run seasons and one 30 home run season.

7 Danny Ainge

Originally a second baseman for the Toronto Blue Jays, Danny Ainge had a respectable, if short, three-year career with a .220 batting average. He then decided to pursue basketball, having made a name for himself on Brigham Young's 1981 NCAA basketball team. Ainge was selected by the Celtics, where he became a two-time NBA Champion in 1984 and 1986, as well as an All Star in 1988.

8 Tim Duncan

Not only one of the best centers ever, Tim Duncan is also one of the best basketball players of all time: a four-time NBA Champion, two-time MVP, and 13-time All Star. There have not been many players of Duncan's caliber—although basketball was Duncan's second choice. He was forced to abandon competitive swimming after a hurricane destroyed his town's only Olympic-sized pool.

9 Brock Lesnar

Known primarily for his career as a professional wrestler with the WWE, Lesnar has also had an impressive career outside of the ring. Not only did he play briefly with the Minnesota Vikings, but he was also an incredibly skilled MMA fighter, at one point being ranked #1 as well as being an Undisputed Heavyweight Champion.

10 Tom Zbikowski

Zbikowski is an NFL safety and a former standout at the University of Notre Dame. His pro career is respectable, if a little unremarkable. However, when he is not playing in the secondary for the Indianapolis Colts, Zbikowski is also an undefeated cruiser weight who has knocked out three of his four opponents.

SOURCES

Alexa Internet (www.alexa.com)

Animal Planet

Art Newspaper

Association of Magazine Media

Badminton World Federation

baseball-reference.com

Baseball Almanac

Beer Tutor

BeerAdvocate

Beerpulse

Best Vodka

Beverage-Digest

Beverage World

Box Office Mojo

Business Insider

cdc.gov/nchs

Centers for Disease Control and Prevention

CIA World Factbook

Congressional Medal of Honor Society

Consumer Product Safetly Council CPSC

Daily Livestock Report

Dayton Business Journal

Euromonitor International

Federal Bureau of Investigation

Food and Agriculture Organization of the United Nations

Global Aircraft

Google

Google via todaynewz.com

go RVing

Guinness Book of Records

Healthline Networks via mobihealthnews.com

Heisman

Hockey-reference.com

Howstuffworks

Huffington Post

iCohol

The Internet Movie Database

Insider Monkey

Institute for Health Metrics and Evaluation at the University of Washington

Interbrand

International Labour Organization of the United Nations

International Trade Administration Manufacturing and Services

itsallgooditgo.com

IUCN/SSC Primate Specialist Group

Listverse

Live Science

MLB.com

Mental Floss

Metacritic

MMOData.net

Mother Nature Network

Movie Body Counts

My Les Paul

NBA Universe (nbauniverse.com)

National Basketball Association

National Climatic Data Center

National Hockey League

National Vital Statistics Report

National Geographic

National Hurricane Center

Nielson BookScan US

QSR magazine

Pro-football-reference.com

ScienceDaily

Southwest Windpower

The Silver Institute

tigerwoods.com

Trust for America's Health

Twitterholic

United Nations MDG Indicators

The Universe Data

University of Michigan Museum of
Zoology

US Census

US Centers for Disease Control and
Prevention

US Department of Agriculture

US Department of Labor

US Energy Information Administration
(EIA)

US Senate

US Social Security Administration

Weather.com

World Christian Database

World Health Organization

World Metro Database

Worldmostexpensive.com

World Tourism Organization

YouTube

The authors gratefully acknowledge the permission granted to reproduce the copyright material in this book. Every effort has been made to trace copyright holders and to obtain their permission for the use of copyright material. The publisher apologizes for any errors or omissions in the above list and would be grateful if notified of any corrections that should be incorporated in future reprints or editions of this book.

ACKNOWLEDGMENTS

We are grateful to our editors at Octopus: Trevor Davies, Sybella Stephens, Pauline Bache, Ellie Sorelli and Jane Ellis, designer Jeremy Tilston, and Davide Pontirolli for production. Thank you for the opportunity, the guidance, the vigilance, and the support. Many thanks also, to Russell's family, for supplementing our research with his, and entrusting us with this work.